HARNESSING THOUGHT

THE GUIDE DOG
A Thinking Animal
with a Skilful Mind

Bruce Johnston

Psychology and Training Consultant
The Guide Dogs for the Blind Association

Lennard Publishing

In memory of

Mike Csernovits

whose insatiable desire to understand
and learn from all the dogs he trained
continues to be an inspiration

———————

First published in 1995 by
Lennard Publishing
a division of
Lennard Associates Limited
Mackerye End, Harpenden
Herts AL5 5DR

The Guide Dogs for the Blind Association
Hillfields, Burghfield, Reading
Berks RG7 3YG

A catalogue entry is available from the British Library

ISBN 1 85291 124 7

Photographs by Robert Digings
All other illustrations by Delaney Communications
Design by Paul Cooper
Edited by Elizabeth Pritchard
Reproduction by Leaside Graphics

Printed and bound in UAE

Contents

TABLE OF PHOTOGRAPHS

TABLE OF FIGURES

Preface

This book tries to give a psychological insight into the skilful and thoughtful mind of the guide dog. By harnessing the dog's thinking, decision making and problem solving abilities many thousands of visually impaired people have been given the opportunity for independent mobility. How does the young dog acquire the knowledge and skills to be a safe, fluent and confident guide? It is a question that takes us to the very forefront of our understanding of animal learning, consciousness and thought

In the wake of the cognitive revolution in human psychology during the past three decades, an interest in animal minds has developed. Previously, psychology in its pursuit of scientific objectivity, felt it necessary to quash any question concerned with the nature of animal mentality. Behaviourism, the most influential school of psychology in the inter-war years, asserted *animals do not think.* Such was the success of the campaign to rid psychology of any mentalistic explanations of behaviour, just about everyone came to believe very little of importance went on in animal minds. Even very complex behaviour by animals was viewed as the product of mechanistic and unthinking processes.

Little heed was taken of Tolman in the 1930s when he suggested processes taking place within the brains of animals were fundamental in helping them guide and plan their actions in the world. Although much of the dogma of behaviourism has now been abandoned, many still find the notion of animals guiding their actions by conscious thought disquieting.

These are critical issues, as the beliefs we hold about the dog's abilities will affect the way we think it ought to be trained. Is the dog capable of taking conscious decisions about alternative courses of action, predicting what is likely to happen next in a particular situation and of remembering how to respond to a wide variety of objects, people and events? For safe and effective work the guide dog has to be rather more than a well trained robot. It is a thinking animal with a skilful mind.

I hope *Harnessing Thought* will be of value to students of psychology and animal behaviour, those with an involvement in animal training and anyone who just wants to understand how the guide dog does its job. It might even be of interest to those researchers in the field of artificial intelligence who have aspirations to design a guiding robot! The purpose of the comprehensive glossary and style of presentation is to make the book accessible to as wide a readership as possible. Time alone will tell whether or not I have been successful.

I am indebted to all at the Middlesbrough Regional Training Centre for their support over the past year and for enabling Alberto Alvarez and Paul Wilson to work alongside me within the Guide Dog Development Unit. Their training skills have helped to further our understanding of canine learning and of a *cognitive* and *holistic* approach to training.

My love and thanks to Jane for all the hours she has spent listening to my ideas and for her many thoughtful and diligent readings of the manuscript. To Heidi Dobie, my sincere appreciation of her secretarial talents and exceptional patience revealed throughout the compilation of the book. My thanks to Robert Digings for his splendid photography achieved over many painstaking hours, and to Mike Delaney and his staff for the excellent illustrations.

Finally, my thanks to my guide dogs over the past 30 years, Cindy, Toni, Binley and Pippa. It is from their skilful and thoughtful behaviour I have learned so much.

Bruce Johnston
March, 1995

CHAPTER ONE
Knowing When and How to Take Decisions

Imagine for a moment walking to your local shopping centre. Reflect upon some of the attentional, visual, memory and movement tasks you perform to enable you to go and return safely. You will need to perceive kerbs, pavements, roads, traffic signs and street furniture, whilst making relatively accurate estimates of the direction and speed of people and vehicle traffic. If you are to complete the trip safely and efficiently you will also need to attend selectively to 'task significant' objects and events, recognise them for what they are and respond accordingly. At the same time you will need to draw upon your spatial map of the area, held within your long-term memory, to know where you are. If you do forget, a quick visual check should be sufficient to restore your orientation.

Now think of yourself travelling by foot in a strange city. Your general knowledge of street objects, people and motor traffic should enable you to get safely from place to place, but at busy road junctions you would be well advised to take your time. The knowledge you have about traffic behaviour in your home area may not apply here. Your spatial map of the city is only in embryonic form and the demand placed upon your attentional, perceptual and memory systems is significantly raised. As you seek to orientate yourself you may find the occasional kerb is missed, the green-man crossing signal appears and passes unnoticed, and people who clearly know where they are going bump into you. You might feel somewhat stressed and this will in turn depress your mobility and orientation skills.

1a *That's a clever girl.*

The purpose of asking you to take these two imaginary journeys is not primarily to demonstrate the central role vision plays in mobility, but rather to highlight the skills of the guide dog. Think of those two journeys again, but this time the traveller is a blind person with his or her guide dog. Now it is the guide dog that has to employ many of the attentional, visual, memory and movement skills if the blind person is to be guided safely through town and city. It is the *dog* which sees lamp posts and avoids them, stops at down-kerbs and finds the road crossing points, stairs and doors to shops and trains when asked to do so (photograph 1a). It is the *dog* which guides the blind person around people, prams and street furniture. And it is the *dog* which helps the guide dog owner know when it is safe to cross the road.

"Find the button Pippa. What a clever girl!"

She stops close to the button for the pelican crossing and turns slightly to her left. This clever positional manoeuvre allows me to press the button without having to stretch awkwardly. She moves positively to the kerb edge at the centre of the crossing and sits. Immediately the audible crossing signal beeps, and sometimes a little before as she sees the traffic has stopped, she crosses in a straight line to the up-kerb (photograph 1b). We normally turn left on the up-kerb. If Pippa does anticipate the left turn before the road crossing has been completed, a quiet but firm "keep straight" will bring us back in line. There are many rules of behaviour we both must keep if we are to remain safe, and crossing roads in a straight line (wherever possible), is one such rule.

1b *In a straight line from kerb to kerb.*

There are a number of roads we have to cross before we reach our destination, a university where students of all ages are helped to develop their thinking, problem solving and decision making skills. Four of them are main roads. We have to find yet more control buttons. If only planners would put them on posts of a similar height and at a standard distance from the kerb edge, life would be so much easier for us both – but perhaps not so much fun. Dogs, as with people, like problems to solve, and some of the buttons we try to hit on the move.

But how do we solve the problem of crossing one of the main roads without the help of a convenient pelican crossing? With a flick of my fingers Pippa turns to her right and sits at the kerb edge. If a vehicle is parked on the other side of the road, preventing a straight crossing, Pippa will continue along the pavement until she reaches a point where the road can be crossed directly.

> *"Thanks Pippa, you have certainly grasped the rule that roads must be crossed in a straight line."*

Not having to manoeuvre around a parked vehicle whilst in the middle of the road makes road crossing much safer!

> *"Well done Pippa. Now you have achieved such a good understanding of what the job is all about, it is important I keep my interference with your work to a minimum and support the decisions you take."*

But what about that moving traffic? I will have more to say later about the guide dog's traffic skills. For now, let us note that if Pippa and I are to cross roads safely, Pippa will need, at an absolute minimum, to judge the position, direction and speed of both near and far traffic. Near traffic is in the lane closest to the guide dog team and far traffic is in the lane on the opposite side of the road. As drivers and pedestrians alike will know to their cost, near and far traffic do not always remain that way! It is just one more difficulty with which the guide dog has to cope.

As we wait at the kerb edge in preparation for crossing, I will be listening and Pippa will be both looking *and* listening. I will be on the ball of my left foot with it placed slightly ahead of my right – communicating to Pippa I am ready to go when we both agree all the conditions for a safe crossing are satisfied. Crossing roads is very much a *team* effort. Pippa's experience has given her an awareness of traffic, an understanding of its behaviour and an appreciation of what she has to do in its presence.

Up a flight of steps, through three sets of doors, across a foyer filled with students and staff and eventually Pippa and I reach another interesting choice point. This time it is between one of two sets of buttons and between one of three lifts. Pippa takes me to the nearest button if there is no lift available with its doors open. If we have to wait she will listen carefully and move towards the next lift expected to arrive on the ground floor. Pippa knows what my intentions are once we have stopped outside the lifts. She does not wait for me to give the command "find the lift", but moves immediately our path is clear. If I had restrained her and only allowed her to move forward after I had given her a command, she would not have learned this helpful skill.

After meeting with a friend and a quick visit to the library, we return to the lift. On arriving at the ground floor, Pippa moves towards the doors even before they open. How does she know we are on the ground floor? I guess by the use of her highly developed sense of smell, with perhaps a little help from distinctive sounds. She leaves the lift with purposeful intent.

"You usually get it right Pippa. The thought of a free run and a game in the nearby park are powerful reasons for you to learn to predict what is likely to happen next."

All work and no play would make the guide dog a dull animal. Play provides stimulation and enjoyment for the dog when off duty. It acts as a potent reinforcer for the work itself and helps strengthen the attachment relationship between dog and owner. Play also offers all dogs the opportunity for the playful practice of small sequences of behaviour which are later combined into the skilled activities of tracking, hunting, fighting and so forth. The two dogs in photograph 1c on the next page, Pippa and Banffy, the family's twelve year old pet Cairn terrier, are play-fighting with their rubber ring. By means of their posture, tail

1c *This is play and it is fun!*

position, growling noises, bodily and facial movements, they will have communicated to one another *this is play*. When I signal to them, with a grasping and pulling movement of my hand, that I am willing to join in their game, they will come over and together present the ring to me.

We need to capitalize on the dog's ability to learn through play. Even the training for the guiding work itself should be provided within an ambience of playfulness. Learning for the guide dog should be fun. We have selectively bred to preserve playfulness in our dogs, that is we have neotenized them. It would be foolish of us not to fully utilize the dog's potential for learning through play. A point succinctly put by Jerome Bruner (1975) when he wrote,

The animal with a rich history of play has prepared himself to be an opportunist. He is able to solve the problems he faces in both an organized and flexible way.

By seeking to preserve playfulness in the dog, we have managed to maintain those mental capacities for curiosity, exploration and problem solving. Throughout the dog's life, but particularly during the early months and years, it is important we nurture

1d *Finding the hand that throws the ball.*

the dog's playfulness, rather than strive to accelerate its obsolescence.

When I go to train with a new dog I always like to take with me a rubber ring or bone. Once the dog knows the toy is theirs, I place it in the bottom drawer of a dressing table and close it leaving sufficient space to insert a paw, but not a head. Binley, my previous guide dog, a Border Collie, was quite some problem solver. He took only a few minutes to realize a paw inserted from the front and gently drawn backwards was the solution. Pippa was equally adept. Although somewhat nervous of touching furniture, only a couple of demonstrations of how the drawer slid back and forth were sufficient for her to solve the problem. She continues to show she is an attentive observer in all situations, even when at play. Just look at her in photographs 1d and 1e putting her ball into the palms of my cupped hands. It does not matter

1e *Here's the ball!*

whether my hands are held close to the ground or at chest height. She will still find them, for she knows exactly what she wants to do, and now has the skill to achieve her intended goal. Of course I will never pick the ball up off the ground, that would be far too easy for Pippa and certainly quite a bother for me. She knows I will only throw the ball for her to chase once it is in the palm of my hand. Even at play the dog is rewarded for making the correct decisions.

Enough of play for the moment. Back to an examination of the complexity of the guiding work itself. To guide a blind person from place to place safely, fluently and comfortably, is indeed a most difficult task. Perhaps it is the most demanding work the human being asks of any animal. And it is a job the dog is expected to do willingly and efficiently, day in and day out, over a number of years.

Clearly, the skilful behaviours displayed by the guide dog are not wired into the animal's brain from birth, nor will they emerge naturally as a result of maturation. That is to say, the guiding behaviours will not develop merely as the dog grows older. No, they have to be acquired by learning and practice. I am sure you have little difficulty in accepting the guide dog has to learn to do its job. That is what training is all about. But what of the notion that the dog has the mental capacity to think and take conscious decisions about alternative courses of action? Now we are entering contentious waters. Have we not been told by most students of animal behaviour, the important mental phenomenon we call *thinking* only occurs in human beings? As the cognitive ethologist, Donald Griffin (1984) points out,

Most biologists and psychologists tend, either explicitly or implicitly, to treat most of the world's animals as mechanisms, complex mechanisms to be sure, but unthinking robots nonetheless.

The guide dog is above all a skilled decision maker, and correct decisions, particularly within an ever changing environment,

1f *What a lot to think about.*

cannot be made without thought. Just ask yourself whether you think the guide dog could really do its job efficiently if it were merely a mechanistic robot without the ability to know when and how to take decisions. I am not asking you to indulge yourself in an anthropomorphic exercise. Rather I am asking you to consider carefully what features of the environment the guide dog has to attend to and think about. Of course, I have no way of knowing what my dogs are really thinking, but I am getting a clearer idea of what they have to think about as they guide me around the streets of my home town.

Have a look at photograph 1f. It was taken with a wide angle lens with the camera placed alongside Pippa's nose as she looked up the street towards the oncoming traffic. To which visual events should she attend? There are many possibilities, even in this still picture in which all movement has been frozen. I am not suggesting either a dog or ourselves have pictures inside our heads. Mammalian brains simply do not work that way. The camera is neither capable of seeing nor being selective in what it captures. Seeing objects and people may seem to be an easy process, yet when computer engineers gave robots artificial vision systems so they could move around in the world, they quickly realized how difficult it is to get them to *really see*. It is Pippa's brain which has to disentangle the vast amount of information hitting her eyes and other sense organs, and it does it far more efficiently than any computer system. To be sure, the eye itself is an optical instrument, but it is the brain which converts electrical impulses from the eye into meaningful patterns which enable her to plan her actions and control her movements. Even so, the photograph of the busy street scene should give you some idea of what she has to attend to and think about when crossing roads. Most of the visual and auditory information reaching her eyes and ears has to be filtered out. Without some form of filtering system between the sense organs themselves and central areas of the brain where seeing and hearing actually take place, the dog's processing system would break down as it became swamped with just too much information. Pippa needs to attend specifically to the position, speed and direction of the vehicles on the road. Even the movements of the pedestrians on the pavements will need to be ignored. Their behaviour is quite superfluous to the task in hand. Pippa can no more afford to let her attention wander than can the car driver when coping with busy traffic conditions, no matter how attractive the dog or person strolling down the pavement might be.

"Are you paying attention to what I say Pippa?"

The guide dog and human operator alike must learn not to respond to events which are irrelevant to the task. Pippa may chase after her ball in the park, but she must never attempt to go after a ball when working. Being a guide dog does seem to be very much concerned with knowing *when* and *how* to take decisions.

CHAPTER TWO
Mechanistic Robot or a Thinking Animal?

The train drew into the station at Stowmarket on a hot summer afternoon in 1975. I was travelling with my German Shepherd guide dog, Toni, and we had to change trains there on our way home from Norwich. I opened the carriage door. "Up hup Toni. Out you go my boy". He turned his large frame across in front of the open door and pushed the side of his body against my legs. "Good thinking", I said to him as I stroked his neck. Getting off a train without the aid of a platform can be a dangerous business! We moved quickly to the door of the next carriage. A brief glance was sufficient for Toni to weigh up the situation. He immediately stepped back away from the open door. One more carriage towards the rear of the train and the problem was solved. With Toni leading the way, we alighted from the train onto a reassuringly solid platform. "Clever boy", I told him. Both of us, still in one piece, duly caught our connection to Bury St. Edmunds.

You would be forgiven for thinking there is nothing very remarkable about the way Toni behaved in this situation. All animals, including humans, have inherited reflexive systems designed to protect them against physical danger. Just note how quickly you remove your hand from a hot ring on the kitchen stove. Although a six foot drop would have presented little difficulty for a large German Shepherd dog, Toni was doing more than responding reflexively to protect himself from possible physical harm. He not only blocked my passage to the open door, but also gently pushed me away from it. It was a unique situation for us both and one in which decisions had to be taken quickly.

Little, if any, thinking is required to get a dog or ourselves to draw away from a painful or frightening event. It is a quick and automatic response. But the clue to ours and many other animals' survival does not lie in a simple reflexive withdrawal from a painful stimulus. Rather the clue lies in the ability of animals to think about the situation and anticipate events before they happen. Yes, thinking is necessary if the painful event is to be avoided in the first place. Was our survival at Stowmarket, some twenty years ago, not dependent upon Toni consciously thinking about what he was doing? He did not appear to be operating like an unthinking automaton. The very survival of animals in the wild would seem to rely on them understanding which sights, sounds and smells forewarn of danger and which signs herald the possibility of food, a drink or a mate. Both wild and domesticated animals seem to be capable of thought.

So how has the view of animals as unthinking robots come about? It had become fashionable in psychology by the 1940s to explain behaviour in terms of observable events. The inter-war years were the grand or infamous era, depending on your point of view, of stimulus-response psychology. Explanations of behaviour were sought in the relationship between events in the environment, termed stimuli, and the animal's response to them. The main interest of the stimulus-response (S-R) psychologists was in the explanation of how animals learned to make new responses to particular stimuli within their environment. Learning new responses was seen as the way the animal in the wild adapted its behaviour in order to survive. What is important to note is this explanation of learning did not find the need to assume that any mental activity akin to thinking or reasoning went on in the animal's brain. The link between the perception of stimulus objects and the animal's behavioural response to them was viewed as being direct. The behaviours displayed by the guide dog would be, in today's terminology, explained away as the product of an input-output system, with the dog's brain serving only to make and maintain the connections between the stimulus and the response. Is it really that easy and straightforward to be a guide dog?

"Don't fret Pippa, we will find a way of allowing you to continue to be a thinking animal."

However, we will be quite unable to derive any comfort from the work of the experimental psychologist, Edward Thorndike. Writing at the turn of the century, he claimed animals were incapable of thinking about what they were doing. Even the cat when it learned to manipulate a complicated series of wheels and pulleys in order to escape from his notorious 'puzzle box' to get to the reward of a piece of fish, was not credited by Thorndike with 'knowing' how it came to solve the problem. He saw learning as a purely automatic process. New stimulus-response connections were merely 'stamped in' when the animal accidentally hit upon the correct solution by a 'trial and error' learning procedure. No mental activity by the animal was required. The new reflexive associations were seen as being formed as a direct result of the effects the response produced. If the outcome of the response had produced effects that were 'satisfying' to the animal, then the bond between the stimulus and the response was strengthened. According to Thorndike, as a connection was strengthened, so the response was more likely to be repeated in the future.

It was a highly mechanistic model of animal learning and one that did not see the animal as having to think consciously about what it was doing. Thinking and reasoning were the preserve of human, and possibly primate brains, and not of animal brains like those of Toni and Pippa. Thorndike considered animals to be basically stupid. A strange consideration for a man who went on to apply his findings from his animal studies to human learning and education.

Now I guess we all have acquired useful skills as a result of 'trial and error' learning. Whether driving, decorating or drawing, those actions that produce the results we desire are noted and repeated. Similarly, I am sure my dogs have picked up a few tricks-of-their-trade by trying out different ways of doing things. As we will see, Binley even hit upon the idea of achieving his goal by walking backwards! No, the main criticism of Thorndike's theory is not with his notion that animals tend to repeat those behaviours which have a positive pay off for them, but rather with his conclusion that no mental activity was required for such learning.

Yet an even heavier gun in the form of behaviourism was waiting to be fired against the idea of *thinking animals*. Considerable blame for the continued emergence of the view of animals as unthinking robots can certainly be laid at the door of John Watson, the founding father of American behaviourism, and on those who have followed in his footsteps.

Behaviourism, which concerned itself mostly with the study of animals in the laboratory, also put forward the proposition that animals do not think. Such was the enthusiasm of the school of behaviourism to develop a truly objective science of psychology, it sought to deny the mental capacity of thinking even to people. Watson went so far as to relegate the mental process of thinking in humans to sub-vocal speech tremors in the larynx. For Watson, only those behaviours that could be observed directly could provide the raw data on which a science of psychology could be built. Provided there was a machine that could measure them, brain waves, pulse rates, lever presses and reaction times were all accepted by behaviourists as objective observations. It did not seem to matter whether or not the data so collected was meaningful, the pursuit of scientific objectivity, however illusory, was everything. Although it is accepted today that a knowledge of the processes taking place within the brains of people and animals is of immense value for understanding their behaviour, any theorising about mental phenomena was a 'no-go area' for behaviourism.

And there were also the findings of Ivan Pavlov, the Russian physiologist, on which Watson could draw to give credence to the developing dogma. Pavlov, working at the turn of the century on the nervous control of digestion in dogs, discovered the conditioned reflex. What was interesting from his work was the dogs did not only salivate automatically to the sight or smell of food, but also to the sound of a ticking metronome, or any other event that had been previously linked with the giving of food. The dogs seemingly had learned that certain sights and sounds signalled the possibility of food. Pavlov believed he had discovered the secret of animal learning. He suggested animals required two types of reflex for their survival in the wild, a group that was inherited, like the knee jerk and unconditioned salivary response, and those that were acquired by learning. Both were seen to operate automatically and unconsciously. Was it a simple form of learning without thought?

Watson saw in Pavlov's discovery of the conditioned reflex, a mechanism that could explain both human and animal learning. And most importantly for Watson's purpose, it provided a way to explain observable behaviour without recourse to mental events such as thinking. He believed he could explain human behaviour as a result of an infinite number of conditionings. There was little hope that behaviourists would find their way to endow non-human animals with thought if they felt they could explain human behaviour without the need to appeal to events taking place within the brains or minds of people.

Watson clearly overstated his case and many of the claims of behaviourism in regard to explanations of animal and human behaviour were wrong. If it were not for the influence of behaviourism on mainstream psychology, particularly during the inter-war years and the early period following World War II, much of what the early behaviourists had to say would be of purely historical interest. But by no means was the impact of behaviourism on psychology entirely negative. Since it was believed findings from the animal laboratory could be used to provide explanations of human behaviour, interest in animal behaviour for its own sake, and in animal learning in particular, was stimulated.

Of special value has been the research of the radical behaviourist, Burrhus Skinner. The principles and procedures contained within his operant learning framework, especially those concerned with the shaping of specific guiding behaviours by the use of positive reinforcers, avoidance learning and extinction, are fundamental for guide dog training. Operantly acquired responses are the building blocks of skilled action by the guide dog. Until his death in 1989, Skinner remained the leading figure of modern behaviourism. But he too fought hard to keep the antimentalistic flag of behaviourism flying. He viewed any questions about the supposed mental states of organisms as improper. Sequences of behaviour in animals were explained away as a chain of reflexes like those used in swallowing or postural adjustment. I am quite sure Skinner would not have explained Toni's behaviour on the train at Stowmarket in terms of him 'knowing' (in any sense of the word) what he was doing. To suggest Toni was conscious of what he was doing implies he was capable of attending to internal images in his brain that represented the relationship between objects and events in that situation.

We too have an enormous range of mental images or internal representations stored within our brains that guide our actions in the world. For example, we employ these internal representations when making a cup of tea, driving a car, eating a meal or merely walking to our local shopping centre. Nevertheless, to infer from its behaviour that an animal has mental images would have been totally unacceptable to Skinner. He made his position quite clear in 1977 by giving the example of a cat chasing a mouse. He views the movements of the cat as very like inherited reflexes. And he warns against inferring there is anything in the cat's brain that corresponds to 'trying to catch the mouse' or even assuming the cat 'likes the chase'.

It seems Skinner would ask me to deny that Pippa knows what she is doing when she chases after her ball in the park and returns it immediately to my hand. And when I find her getting the ball out of the bag as soon as we reach the park, am I not allowed to infer that she enjoys the play? More importantly, am I forced by Skinner to explain the complex actions of the guide dog's work simply as chains of conditioned reflexes? Presumably so, for Skinner is saying that rats, cats, dogs and the like do not have the mental capacity to behave otherwise.

Let us suppose for a moment Skinner is correct in his view that the behaviour of animals is best explained as chains of conditioned reflexes. He may not be far off the mark if he were to describe some aspects of the guide dog's work as the linking of a number of responses into a chain. The chaining of responses is evident as the dog guides along a well known and relatively clear pavement. Even moving to one side of the pavement to avoid lamp posts and other street furniture appears to be carried out relatively automatically. Although well practised movements become less *deliberate* and more *automatic* as the dog becomes more skilful, I hesitate to describe even straight forward obstacle avoidance by the guide dog as merely reflexive. However, for the purpose of the discussion, let us stay with Skinner's explanation and take such behaviours to be purely the result of reflexive conditioning. I then wonder how Skinner would have explained what the guide dog does when the unexpected happens? When the shopping trolley suddenly veers off course or the window shopper unwittingly steps backwards into the path of the guide dog team, does the guide dog somehow unconsciously flick into another set of conditioned reflexes? (See photographs 2a and 2b overleaf.)

Similarly with skilful people, how does the experienced car driver cope when the gear stick jams in neutral? And I must not forget to remind you of Toni when he had to cope with being asked to get off a train without the aid of a platform. No, in all

2a & 2b *Unexpected events have to be dealt with.*

of these cases, and many others, a 'conditioning' framework fails to explain how the guide dog or car driver deals with the unexpected event. In each, conscious decisions are clearly called for. The actions that were being carried out, relatively automatically, have now to occupy the conscious attention of either the skilful dog or human operator. Fortunately, the guide dog does have the mental equipment to deal with the unexpected.

It is reassuring to read Griffin (1991) when he writes,

The investigation of animal cognition and mental experiences is beginning to reveal that animals guide their behaviour by surprisingly complex thinking. The versatile adaptability of some animals in the face of unpredictable challenges suggests simple conscious thinking about alternative actions and their probable results.

Although Griffin is referring to animals in the wild, the guide dog too is frequently faced with having to make conscious choices about alternative courses of action, and some of the decisions that are demanded by the situation are often far from simple!

"Are you feeling a little better now Pippa?"

I am never sure which suffered more from the dogma of behaviourism – the understanding we have of our own behaviour or that of animals. At least people could always answer back and tell the stimulus-response psychologists that human behaviour is far more flexible and thoughtful than they suggest. But animals cannot reply to those who construe their behaviour as unthinking and mechanistic. Although we have rightly discarded many of the views of behaviourism, in so far as they apply to our own behaviour, I fear many psychologists, and non-psychologists alike, find it difficult to escape from the blinkered perspective of behaviourism and attribute to animals the capacity for conscious thought. Is there not still a widespread belief that the behaviour of animals, including dogs, is best explained in broadly mechanistic terms? I think so.

"I am sure we have still some way to go Pippa, before we will convince a number of psychologists, dog trainers and many others that you are a thinking animal and not merely a mechanistic robot. Behaviourism has certainly left its mark. Its influence is revealed in how people so frequently explain away your skilful behaviour as just a series of conditioned responses."

But even as far back as the 1930s the lone voice of the cognitive behaviourist, Edward Tolman, could just be heard proclaiming from within the mental wilderness of behaviourism, animals have some knowledge of where they are in the world, have the ability to anticipate what was likely to happen next in a particular situation and have the mental equipment to enable them to act with a certain degree of purpose. He was suggesting the behaviour of animals might be regulated by inner mental processes, rather than driven by automatic and unconscious reflexes. Tolman was dissatisfied with the mechanistic explanations of animal behaviour being put forward by his behaviourist colleagues. He argued any satisfactory explanation of behaviour would need to take account of the processes taking place within the brains of animals. Tolman did not view animal behaviour as necessarily inflexible and habit bound. He suggested, for example, the goal of obtaining food by the animal would probably remain fixed, but the means of achieving that goal need not. That does not mean animals and ourselves never behave in an unthinking and routine way. I know I find myself doing things out of habit, even though changed circumstances require I should behave differently. Have you not found yourself walking or driving to a place out of habit, even though it was not your intended destination?

Let me recount an episode about Binley. His behaviour, on the occasion I have in mind, could never be construed as being the result of a fixed and unthinking habit. This instructive example of thoughtful and flexible behaviour took place when I was training with Binley in Reading. He was confronted by scaffolding with an archway wide enough for us both to pass through. However, as he approached the scaffolding, the route through became blocked by pedestrians. Binley moved to his right to the outside of the scaffolding (with the road to the right) and was immediately confronted by a lamp post with a previously unsighted bin attached. This situation would have normally demanded an off-kerb procedure with both of us having to go into the busy main road in order to avoid the pavement obstacle. Without prompting, he took three or four paces backwards, turned left and went through the archway which was by then clear for us to pass through safely. The goal of the work remained fixed, but the route to the goal certainly did not! Binley had to think his way through this complex situation. This incident took place after only ten days of us working together, and let me assure you he had not been taught to walk backwards during his previous training! No rigidly formulated stimulus-response theory could ever explain how he came to perform this highly original manoeuvre to attain his intended goal.

Has the trained guide dog the ability to think its way through the work, make conscious choices about alternative courses of action and operate as a problem solver, or is it best viewed as a well conditioned biological machine? The answers to these questions raise important issues for training. The beliefs we hold about the dog's intellectual abilities will affect significantly the manner in which we think it ought to be trained. Should guide dog training be directed towards the production of well conditioned animals, or should it attempt to develop the decision making and problem solving skills of the dog?

CHAPTER THREE

Mental Representations and Canine Cognition

Precisely how we come to represent the world inside our heads has been one of the most fundamental questions in philosophy and human psychology for centuries. Despite the suggestions of Tolman in the 1930s, only recently has the possibility of mental representations in animals become accepted as a *proper* question for science to address. Such was the vigorous opposition of behaviourism to explanations of behaviour in mentalistic terms, any suggestion that animals could have an awareness of what they were doing, operate insightfully or develop expectancies about outcomes, was ignored. But if Pippa is quite unaware of what she is doing,

3a *Time to put your ball in the bag.*

how does she know to drop her ball into the presented bag (photograph 3a) at the end of our walk in the park? Is she really oblivious to the outcomes associated with her own actions?

3b *Missed – have another go.*

If so, I wonder why she gives an expectant wag of her tail as soon as she drops the ball into the bag and before I tell her she is a "clever girl"? A sense of *knowing* by Pippa of what she is doing implies she has the capacity to form and utilize mental representations – images within her brain – to guide her actions in the world. In this simple situation, for Pippa to be successful, she will need to attend to mental images that represent the essential spatial relationships between ball and bag and her own behaviour. She must have some means of representing knowledge of what to do when the stimulus of the open bag is presented. When an animal carries out a behaviour sequence correctly, apparently on the basis of what it has experienced in the past, it would seem very reasonable to assume images of earlier situations are revived to guide current action.

"Yes Pippa, I know from your behaviour you have a good idea, in the form of a mental image, of the goal you are attempting to attain. I also see on the rare occasions you fail to get the ball into the bag, how you immediately pick it up and have another attempt (photograph 3b). You certainly have a clear idea of what you want to do and an understanding of when you have been unsuccessful."

Pippa in this situation, and more essentially when guiding, has continually to check the state of affairs she intends to achieve has been accomplished. She tests the situation, acts and once again tests the situation to ensure she has attained her goal.

And if an example from our own behaviour will help, reflect for a moment upon the mental images we require when attempting to throw a ball into a small container. We too have to have a knowledge of *what* to do and *how* to do it. Or if you prefer an example a little closer to your everyday experience, consider the sequence of internal images or mental schemata you require when making and pouring a cup of tea. We can also appreciate the nature of the mental imagery necessary for the organization of relatively simple physical motor behaviours by observing a young child attempting to build a tower of bricks. Eye-hand coordination, together with a certain level of muscle control, is necessary for success, but the organization of the sequence of the required behaviours is under the control of images inside the infant's brain.

Mental imagery also serves another purpose. For effective navigation through the world, animals and people need a means of laying down memories of the spatial arrangement of significant stimulus objects in their environment. Whether in the north or south of their habitat, it is essential for their survival that animals have a stored knowledge of the location of water holes and food supplies in relation to their current position. The fact that animals can navigate and orientate themselves in space in the pursuit of specific goals, was argued by Tolman to be an indication that animals have the capability to create mental images of their environment in the form of a cognitive map.

The guide dog too forms a memory image of the layout of streets within its work area of town or city. On many occasions I have had cause to be grateful to the cognitive maps formed and stored by my guide dogs. When thinking of other matters I sometimes lose track of exactly where I am. Thankfully, they always know where they are and usually have a good idea of my intended destination. When homeward bound to their den of food and fun, they never seem to doubt where I want to go. It does not matter from which direction I might be returning home, they always know their way.

Interestingly, Nicholas Mackintosh (1984) and Anthony Dickinson (1980), both leading authorities in the field of animal learning, conclude from their research, that the behavioural data of Thorndike and Pavlov on animal learning is best explained by supposing animals develop mental images representing 'expectancies about outcomes'. They have come to share Tolman's dissatisfaction with the explanations of animal learning offered by stimulus-response psychology. They now accept animals would appear to be capable of planning their actions on the basis of anticipated events and of learning that their behaviour has certain consequences. Even a rat learning to press a lever in a Skinner box for a food reward, or a dog salivating to the ticking of a metronome, seem to demand an explanation in terms of the animal being able to form central representations of the anticipated results of its own behaviour or of events in the environment.

It would be difficult to overestimate the significance for the guide dog of being able to think ahead and anticipate the consequences associated with its own actions. Correct decisions can be made only by the dog with the ability to predict the likely outcomes related to alternative courses of action. Learning the skills of guiding will necessarily involve the dog having to store memories of those actions in a particular situation that have a positive pay off for it and those which do not. To learn, and thus profit from past experiences, the guide dog must possess the capacity to record, store and retrieve knowledge of past events. It needs to be able to remember which actions in the past were reinforced with praise and those which were discouraged. Memories of what happened in the past enable the dog to guide its actions in the future.

So can we think of mental images or representations simply as memories of stimulus objects? Yes, to some degree the terms representation and memory can often be used interchangeably, as for example when the representation is of a specific object. The guide dog has to form and retain many memories of tangible things within its brain. Not merely of balls and bags, but more importantly of kerbs and cars, lamp posts and ladders.

However, to talk of the knowledge acquired by the guide dog as always being stored as a straightforward memory of objects could be misleading. Safe and skilful guiding by the dog demands that it acquires and uses knowledge that represents more than simple memories of concrete events. Fundamental for the guiding work is the need for the dog to group stimulus objects together to form a *class*. But once again we find many who would doubt the ability of the dog to group similar things together to form a class or concept, despite the fact this is a mental activity so obvious in ourselves.

The natural tendency we have to divide the world of objects into categories can be observed in the human infant as he or she comes to appreciate the characteristics that make a rattle a rattle, a spoon a spoon and a dog a dog, despite a variation in their size, shape and colour. Classification of the world is essential for our thinking, and so it is for the guide dog. It would be difficult to explain how the guide dog does its job if it did not have the ability to classify stimulus objects and events.

3c *Straightforward*

In photograph 3c you can see

3d *Not so easy.*   **3e** *Quite a problem.*

Pippa has stopped and is sitting correctly at the kerb edge. She must stop at all road kerbs, neither stopping a few inches too short, nor overshooting. And she must also learn to stop at the kerb edge whether it has been lowered for wheelchair users as shown in photograph 3d or even when, if you can follow my meaning, there is no kerb at all and the edge of the road is marked only by a yellow line or shallow gutter (photograph 3e). Pippa has to develop a concept of the 'kerbiness' of kerbs. In other words she must understand what are the features which indicate that a kerb is a kerb, whether it is high, low or flattened.

Similarly when crossing the road, a car, a bus or a bike have to be grouped together as a class of objects such that Pippa can respond to them in the same way. We too have to do the same when crossing roads. Whether it is a car or a bus, the colour or make are immaterial in making a decision when it is safe to cross. What matters is the position, direction of movement and speed of the bus, car or lorry. We have a word to help us classify these 'things' which travel on the road, we label them all as vehicles.

So Pippa has to do more than simply build a memory store of stimulus objects. She has to be able to represent objects and events in her brain in such a way that she can classify and manipulate the stored information to produce effective guiding actions. Her internal representations are the building blocks with which other mental processes such as object recognition, concept formation, thinking and problem solving are constructed. Once formed, these images in the brain constitute the basic units of her cognition.

But what precisely is cognition? At one level it may be thought of as the processes in the brain which enable an animal to gain information about its environment. More broadly, we may take cognition to refer to the existence and utilization of stored representations of knowledge which the animal has, not only about its physical environment, but of people, other animals, and of itself. For the specific work of the guide dog, it will refer to those mental representations of knowledge concerned with the *what* and the *how* of the guiding task. According to a dictionary definition (*Macmillan Dictionary of Psychology*, 1989) the term cognition refers to,

The mental processes concerned with the acquisition and manipulation of knowledge, including perception and thinking.

We can note from this definition that cognition is a *process* and not a *thing*. It is a sequence of interrelated mental events taking place within the brains of animals and people.

So when I write of the dog showing 'intelligence', 'reasoning', 'insight' or merely 'recognizing objects in the world', I am referring to aspects of its cognition. The term cognition is normally used when the behaviour exhibited by an animal in response to environmental stimuli is more than a predictable and automatic reaction. An important feature of the cognitive process is that it intervenes between the incoming sensory data and actions.

But as we have seen, to talk of cognition in animals in this way has not gone unchallenged. Skinner, for example, considered it quite improper to infer that animals have cognitions. What can be said without controversy, is that all animals receive information about the environment through their sense organs (eyes, ears, nose etc.) and in turn exhibit behaviour. The debate is about the existence and nature of the processes occurring within the brain between the reception of sense data and the generation of behaviour. Hopefully, I am well on the way to dispelling any notion that dogs and many other animals are mindless creatures incapable of thought. Dogs really do have cognitions. Without the capability 'to think', the guide dog could never do its job.

Following the invention of the digital computer, it became increasingly fashionable in the 1960s and 1970s to compare the activities taking place within the human mind to the functions of a computer. The mind was viewed as an information processing system. More recently, it is a metaphor which has been usefully applied to the study of cognition in animals. It is a framework that allows us to think of the guide dog with its on-board computer (its brain) receiving, recognizing, classifying, storing, analysing information and emitting behaviours as it thinks its way through the work.

"I guess it is a model that reflects far more accurately what is going on in your head Pippa, than does any stimulus-response theory of your behaviour. But do you think this model of you as an information processing system goes far enough to fully explain your skilful actions?"

It certainly recognizes dogs have cognitions and are capable of translating acquired knowledge into action. Nevertheless, the brain of the dog is more than a computer with the capacity for processing information. Conscious decision making, foresight, reasoning and the utilization of stored information for the production of flexible behaviours are not the characteristics of a computer, but they do represent aspects of the guide dog's biological intelligence. Such features of the dog's cognition are not necessarily encompassed within an information processing model. Valuable as the model has proved to be for the understanding of animal cognition in general, it has its limitations and dangers. For those who so wish, it is a framework which still allows them to provide an explanation of the guide dog's behaviour without attributing to it a conscious awareness or understanding of what it is doing. Griffin (1991) points out,

We tend to find the notion of conscious awareness disturbing and struggle to find ways of analysing animal behaviour without allowing what seem like subversive notions of subjectivity to get a foot in the door.

But can the dogma of behaviourism be blamed entirely for our reluctance to attribute the capacity for conscious thought to animals? No, this conceited notion that only the human animal is conscious of what it is doing is a view that was around a long time before the birth of twentieth century behaviourism. The seventeenth century French philosopher, Rene Descartes, was a particularly influential figure in the emergence of this anthropocentric view of animal behaviour. For him, the human animal was unique in having besides an animal's clockwork brain, a rational soul or mind. A distinguishing feature of that rational soul was the capacity for conscious thought. Cartesian philosophy conceived of the mind as quite separate from the functions of the mechanical brain and body. Human and animal brains alike were viewed as mere machines, responding reflexively to events in the world. The mind was not seen to interfere with the workings of the brain or the brain with the functions of the mind.

The most important question in neurobiology today is

concerned with the relationship between the mind and the brain. Most neuroscientists now believe all aspects of mind, including consciousness, will be ultimately explicable in a materialistic way. Is not my mind, which represents the very essence of my individuality in the way I consciously think and act, the result of the interaction between large sets of nerve cells in my brain? The mind is not a *thing*, rather it is a *process,* a sequence of events within the brain which are responsible for the mental phenomena we call thinking and consciousness.

Even so, a few neuroscientists, such as Sir John Eccles, still maintain the soul is distinct from the body. Not everyone, it would seem, can accept the mind is the product of brain activity. They continue to view the mind as a non-material substance or spirit endowed with the faculty for rational and conscious thought, and possessed only by people.

Nonetheless, I intend to use the term 'mind' to refer to those aspects of brain function concerned with cognition and consciousness in ourselves and animals. So when I write of the 'mind' of the guide dog, I will be referring to those processes in its brain involved with cognition, from the fundamental processes involved in remembering the characteristics of concrete objects to those higher order cognitive activities of decision making and problem solving.

But I must point out the mind is not without emotion. The mind is not a pure cognitive system. Guide dogs are not devoid of feelings! Emotions and cognitive functioning interact in the mind of the guide dog just as they do in the minds of people. For example, emotions like fear can affect the dog's ability to process information effectively and the dog's cognitive constructions of the world can in turn affect the way it responds to events. The latter point is exemplified in the condition termed 'learned helplessness' in which the dog comes to believe (usually as a result of inconsistent punishment) its actions are unconnected to outcomes. For example, it may seem to the dog that whatever it does the outcome is always a punishing one. An understanding of how the emotional and cognitive activities of the guide dog's mind interact will be pertinent to all aspects of the dog's training and work. Emotional factors can both enhance and inhibit performance. Confident decision making by the guide dog is dependent upon both thought and feeling.

And let me try and show you why the commonly held belief that the possession of a spoken language is essential for thought is also false. The emergence of a spoken and written language is probably the single most important factor in the explanation of our phenomenal cultural progress as a species. However, because our thinking seems so intimately bound to language, we are frequently in danger of assuming only animals with speech are capable of thought. We have noted already Watson's ridiculous idea that thinking in human beings could be viewed as merely sub-vocal tremors in the voicebox. He conjectured that thinking by people was just a matter of talking to oneself. Are children during the pre-linguistic stage of their development, and deaf people who cannot speak (or even communicate by hand-sign) to be considered incapable of thought? I think not. And if we were to follow this line of reasoning, which argues language is a prerequisite for thought, are all non-human animals destined to be unthinking robots?

Have a look at figure 1. Amongst this collection of dogs we will quickly recognize there is one cat. How is it we can perform this cognitive analysis and immediately point to the odd one out, despite the fact cats and dogs have many features in common? They both have four legs, a tail, fur and so on. It does not seem to matter whether the dog is large or small, black or brown, with ears that stick up or those that flop down, we still have an internal representation or model of what constitutes the 'doginess' of dogs and the 'catiness' of cats. We are able to check the characteristics of the animals we see in the figure against our internal representations of 'doginess' and 'catiness'. Although we clearly appreciate the salient features of cats and

FIGURE 1 *Spot the odd one out.*

dogs which enable us to classify them differently, we would be hard pressed to express the reasons for our categorisation in words. Language does not seem to be the critical faculty for our classificatory skills.

I always marvel at the wonderful cognitive analysis performed by infants who pass me in their prams and point out to their mum or dad the animal in the white harness is 'a dog'. German shepherd, labrador or collie, large, medium or small, they are always classified correctly as 'a dog', and just occasionally as a 'blind dog'. They know Pippa can *see* really! Language is evidently mapped onto thought, and the infant had begun the important task of dividing the world of objects into categories of cats and dogs and so on, some time before being able to use the correct label.

A very young friend of mine used to classify all animals that moved as 'cows', even the next-door neighbour. Although he soon learned the error of his ways, it was already evident from his behaviour that he appreciated the difference between people and cows, but he had not yet learned the correct word for the various classes of animal. He had formed mental representations of various animals before he had acquired the appropriate matching vocabulary. Even though language gives a tremendous super-charged boost to our ability to classify the world, and communicate that knowledge to others, language is not a prerequisite for categorization and thought.

The guide dog has necessarily to recognize and classify significant objects within its *guiding environment* and anticipate the consequences of its actions in relation to them. Such cognitive manipulation of the stored mental images is achieved without a language to label the various categories. Photographs 3f and 3g picture Pippa dealing with two rather similar pavement obstacles, a ladder and scaffolding respectively. It is imperative she divides these two stimulus events into separate categories as the response required to each is somewhat different.

3f *The 'ladderness' of ladders.*

In photograph 3f Pippa has recognized the ladder for what it is and is following the general rule of never guiding under a ladder. Except on those very rare occasions when there is ample room for both of us to pass under it quite safely, on no account should she choose to go under a ladder. And the rule still applies even if she has to go into the road and treat the ladder as an off-kerb obstacle. Rules of response are related directly to the situation confronting the guide dog. That is why I used the phrase, 'she has recognized the ladder for what it is'. Pippa's understanding of the situation is revealed in the correctness of her behaviour. We demonstrated our ability to grasp the salient features of a *class* in a similar way when we pointed to the cat as the odd one out in figure 1.

Now look what Pippa is doing in photograph 3g. She has decided to guide me through the scaffolding. Different rules apply when negotiating scaffolding compared with ladders. As we saw in the last chapter, Binley even walked backwards because he was so confident it was perfectly all right for him to go through the pavement scaffolding. But he never, to my knowledge, guided me under a ladder in the whole of his working life. He certainly knew how to classify and manipulate his mental representations of the world. In short, he was *thinking* about what he was doing.

Thinking, either in ourselves or other animals, is dependent upon two mental processes. Firstly, the *thinking animal* has to be able to represent the world inside its head and secondly, manipulate mental representations in order to predict the likely outcome of a particular course of action.

Problem solving is very much a matter of jiggling about with mental representations. When elements in the old situation are changed, new actions may have to be taken if a goal is to be reached. I am sure Binley satisfied the above criteria of thinking when he walked backwards in Reading. He was able to step back from the immediate stimulus events, and to adapt a phrase from Sir Frederick Bartlett (1932), 'turn around on his schemata'.

So it would seem whether the guide dog is simply stopping at a lowered kerb or skilfully guiding a blind person through pavement scaffolding, the origin of their thoughtful and safe behaviour is to be found in the cognitive processes operating within their canine brain and mind.

3g *The 'scaffoldness' of scaffolding.*

CHAPTER FOUR
A Biological Intelligence Makes all the Difference

How was I to navigate through the world without the aid of vision? Naturally, that was a question that preoccupied my mind when I first lost my sight in 1963. Initially I was trained in the use of the short white cane. It could be held across the body or tapped along a wall or fence. When simply held across the body it acted more as a signal to others that I was 'on the loose' rather than as an effective mobility aid. To find the edge of a kerb without first dropping into the gutter necessitated the adoption of a bent and inelegant posture. Safe, comfortable and graceful mobility appeared to be a long way off for me. Identifying obstacles at ground level was just a matter of luck. To use the short cane to guide along a wall certainly gave me more information about my immediate environment. At least I knew where I was on the pavement and my speed and posture were much improved, but it too had its problems. To go through the centre of Sheffield in this manner caused many a window shopper to jump with surprise, and I suspect on occasion, with some pain. The long cane would have offered me more information about my immediate environment and it would have helped me to overcome my postural and sadistic problems, but it was only just beginning to be cautiously introduced into this country in the early 1960s. At the time, the guide dog seemed to be the only answer for my independent mobility needs.

Over the past twenty years or more, a variety of electronic sensory aids have been developed to help the blind traveller. To date, they have had only very limited success. These devices emit ultrasound or coherent light and convert the energy

46

reflected from objects into some form of audible or tactile display. Many of them were designed on the premise that what the blind traveller needed above all was more raw (unfiltered) data about his or her environment. It was assumed the blind person would be able to decode the signals bounced back off stationary and moving obstacles.

However, a basic assumption of this research was incorrect. The blind traveller does need to have information about the environment if correct decisions are to be taken, but it must be in a form he or she can deal with quickly. It is quite impossible for the human brain to receive, process and translate the incoming auditory or tactile data into action within the time available. These electronic detectors, as with the camera, are not selective in what they capture. Even if the device is pointed in the right direction to pick up the significant pavement obstacles, the time taken for effective recognition is too long.

What seemed to be required was a system that could not only receive information but also assist in its translation. Could the research in the area of artificial intelligence and the associated applied field of robotics provide a solution? Robots have been designed to make cars, deliver food to patients in hospital and identify enemy tanks – so why not a guiding robot?

The idea of 'thinking machines' was first suggested by Alan Turing in the 1940s. Despite abundant work in the field of artificial intelligence, his ideas and hopes have yet to be realized. No one has yet designed a truly 'thoughtful' and 'intelligent' robot.

"Sleep peacefully in your bed Pippa, confident in the knowledge no robot has yet been designed that could do your job. Computers do not have the quality or flexibility of thought to allow them to solve the problems or take the decisions that are asked of you."

If a guiding robot could be designed to do the job of a guide dog it would have to be programmed to systematically work through an enormous number of complex mathematical equations at each stage of a route. I guess by the time it had worked out how to respond to all the events presented to it on a journey across town all the stars would have gone out!

> *"But you just do it Pippa. You stop at kerbs and go round ladders with ease because you have developed an ability to recognize objects for what they are and to understand what actions are required when you meet with them."*

The 'rules' that govern the guide dog's behaviour operate quite differently from those of a computerized robot. They emanate from its biological intelligence and not from an artificial one – and that makes all the difference!

Even to design a computerized robot that could build a tower of bricks took several years of research. To recognize a building block for what it is, whether viewed in light or shade or tilted at an angle, appears to us to be as easy as pie – but not for a robot with a television camera for an eye, computer hardware for a brain and a software program for its so-called *mind*. One inadequately programmed robot which 'knew' nothing about gravity, even started the building of a tower with the 'top' brick. Of course, it did not remain the 'top' brick for very long!

The cartoon (figure 2) amusingly illustrates the problems faced when attempting to design a robot that could catch a ball thrown against a wall – but the dog (as with an infant building a tower of bricks) just does it. To get a stationary artificial-vision-system to recognize objects quickly and accurately is difficult enough, but to get a moving one to do so has proved to be a nigh intractable problem.

Even if we have not yet been able to design a thinking machine, the work on artificial intelligence has shown us very clearly what a magnificent organ the mammalian brain is in its capacity for transforming information. It is the brain's ability to make sense of data received from the environment and in turn

FIGURE 2 *But I just do it!*

integrate such information with stored knowledge in the production of appropriate behaviour that is so outstanding.

Many of the early workers in the field of artificial intelligence argued it was unnecessary to know how the brain worked in order to get a machine to think, just as it had proved unnecessary to give a machine flapping wings in order to get it to fly. Other researchers, however, never accepted that thinking could ever occur within a machine unless first an artificial brain was constructed. By imitating nature, would it be possible to get an artificial brain to learn and acquire concepts? That was the hope of groups of workers in the 1950s who became known as connectionists.

During this early period they built a few working Perceptrons as these artificial brains were called. As an example of what they could do, after a number of presentations of male and female faces they were able to distinguish between them. Specific 'experiences' with faces had brought about changes in the strength of the connections within the nerve network such that specific features that constituted the maleness or femaleness of faces could be discriminated. Although it was difficult to know which features it would extract as representative of a class, it had demonstrated it could acquire concepts of a sort.

But after a promising beginning this approach to machine intelligence virtually died out. However, in the 1970s as research problems into artificial intelligence seemed insurmountable, connectionism underwent a revival with modern Perceptrons now being called neural networks. Connectionism is a synonym for parallel distributed processing (PDP), so-called because more than one input is involved in the formation of the connections within the nerve net.

Real brains too, probably process information in parallel. Early ideas on cognitive processing, for example by Donald Broadbent (1958), proposed a linear flow of information in which the incoming data was transformed in a series of discrete stages beginning with sense reception and ending with long-term memory and/or motor output. More recent ideas, particularly the models constructed by connectionists, attempt to represent the greater complexity of information processing in biological brains by incorporating such a feature as parallel processing into the system.

Some of these new nerve net systems have been able to classify the incoming information in interesting ways and form what appear to be new concepts. So are we getting a little closer to creating something like a biological brain and mind? Some believe these nerve networks mark one of the most important steps forward in our understanding of the brain processes which underpin the activities of the mind.

Connectionists all over the world are trying to find out what their nerve nets can learn. While networks are appealing, the small tasks they are able to conquer are a far cry from the integrated *commonsense* knowledge acquired by human and animal brains. One such robotic nerve net had to be retrained when it rained, as it could not recognize objects for what they were under these altered conditions. It is still a problem to know which features from their 'experiences' such nerve nets are likely to extract as they attempt to form concepts. They certainly have no understanding of what they are doing.

"No such problems with you Pippa, although I have noted your preference for working in the dry rather than the rain. But how clever you were when you still stopped at the kerb edge even though it had been obliterated by snow. That shows a flexibility and an understanding that cannot be matched by any artificial intelligence. You seem to have acquired a 'commonsense' knowledge of your work."

To get nerve nets to capture something as fundamental as *commonsense* behaviour seems a long way off. Connectionism has made a start. Nerve networks have been able to recognize simple patterns and navigate (to a limited extent) through the

matter whether the letter is a capital or lower case, printed or written, large or small or even presented on its side – we still recognize the letter 't' as a 't'. It is impossible to conceive of a template based recognition system that could cope with all these variations. The templates that would be required to enable us to identify correctly all letters, irrespective of their size, orientation or form of presentation, would be enormous and prohibitive. A template-matching explanation of pattern recognition is unsatisfactory, at least in people, but I suspect the same is true for the dog. Scaffolding, kerbs and vehicles also come in all shapes and sizes.

"Yes, it is the same for you too Pippa. An explanation of your ability to recognize objects in terms of template-matching would be inadequate. I cannot see how such a model of your pattern recognition could account for the speed of your decision making or the flexibility you show in your behaviour. I will always remember on your first visit to the shopping precinct in Ipswich how you immediately knew it was alright to use its entire width in order to ensure our speedy progress, yet it was only in some ways like the shopping precinct you had experienced whilst undergoing training at Middlesbrough. I am sure you do not have a set of templates in your brain which represent all possible forms of precinct! It is when attempting to explain how you recognize an object like a building or a precinct, which belongs to a broad and ill-defined category, that the shortcomings of template-matching theories are revealed most starkly."

Neither would a template-matching theory explain how we are able to recognize a cat in the midst of a group of dogs as was illustrated in figure 1.

However, if we look at the braille word processor and the personal reader, we will find their recognition systems are based on a form of template-matching. For example, if I were to type into the braille word processor the words 'goide dog' rather than 'guide dog', then, as you can see (or perhaps you did not notice) the incorrect spelling of 'guide' is faithfully reproduced in the hard copy print version you are now reading. Figure 5 illustrates how simply typing dot 5 instead of dot 6 changes 'u' into 'o'. It is the same principle that operates when you enter your personal number at a cash point to match the code on your card.

The problems faced by a template-matching system as an explanation of pattern recognition in humans may be revealed further by looking at the pattern recognition system of the personal reader. You will remember the personal reader is a machine that contains a camera that scans a book and translates the printed material into speech or braille. It too has a recognition system which is based on a form of template-matching. Excellent though the machine is, it has its limitations. It can only read printed material that is well-defined. If the letters touch one another such that no space between the letters can be detected, the machine will report, 'unrecognized character'. The template nature of its pattern recognition system is unable to cope with any pattern which is not stored within its memory. Not surprisingly, it also confuses similar shaped letters and numbers. Because it compares the image received from the camera with a set of templates, it sometimes fails to discriminate accurately between, for example, the letter 'S' and the number '5', the letter '*l*' and the number '1' and the letters 'O' and 'D' etc. It has no understanding of what it is reading, and unlike you and I, cannot make *an effort after meaning*. I am sure you will have no difficulty reading the following sentences despite the fact I have substituted an 'x' for some of the letters.

FIGURE 5

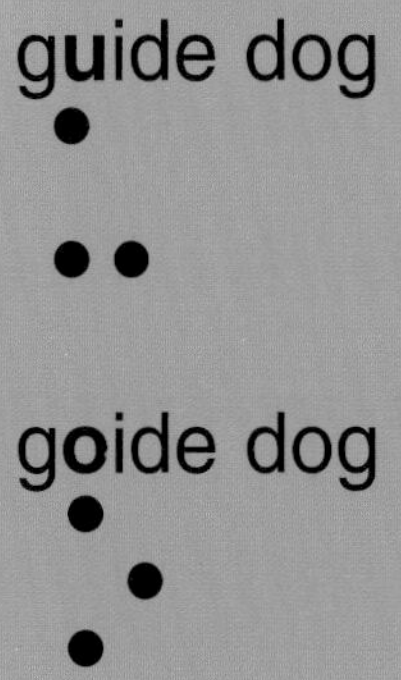

guide dog

goide dog

Typing dot 5 instead of dot 6 in the U of guide dog produces goide dog rather than guide dog.

Txe lady placxd the xreath of flowexs on thx table.
The xheel felx ofx the lorry.

You understand the meaning of words within the context of a sentence, a paragraph and so on. Context cues allow you to recognize the meaning of words and sentences quickly and accurately. Context cues are also important in helping Pippa to recognize patterns, discriminate between objects and understand the 'meaning' and significance of objects in relation to her guiding behaviour.

Template-matching seems unable to explain satisfactorily pattern recognition in ourselves or the dog. Have any alternative explanations of pattern recognition been put forward? Yes, two other rather similar theories have been proposed and both are better able to account for the versatility and complexity of perceptual processing than a template-matching model. They are *prototype* and *feature* theories.

Prototype theories view pattern recognition as a process involving the extraction of key attributes from a stimulus and their comparison with an abstract representation of that stimulus held in long-term memory. Such representations are called prototypes. Prototypes represent the most basic and essential form of the stimulus. Just sufficient information to define its class membership. Thus, for example, a prototypical dog might be represented by a cylindrical tube for the body, a 'stick' at each corner for the legs, a sphere for the head and so on. (Some prefer the term 'knowledge schema' to refer to this organized representation.) One advantage of prototype theories compared with template-matching theories is clear. The information that has to be stored in long-term memory is much less – a manageable number of prototypes rather than an infinite number of templates.

Although prototype theories are far superior to models based on template-matching in their ability to explain satisfactorily pattern recognition in people and animals, they too have their limitations. For example, they are not explicit in how the match is made between the internal representation of a stimulus and a prototype. Does the matching process occur serially (one after another) or in parallel (more than one at a time)? If it were the former, pattern recognition would take too much time, and we know this is not the case. Speed of decision making is critical in many aspects of the guide dog's work, none more so than when having to deal with a whole series of stimulus events simultaneously, as when crossing a road. Pattern recognition must be dependent on information being processed in parallel and interpreted through some form of schematic representation. Furthermore, prototype theories fail to explain how pattern recognition is crucially dependent on the context in which a stimulus is encountered. It is not just the characteristics of the stimulus that are crucial for the accurate recognition of objects.

Even though feature theories also fail to explain satisfactorily the important role played by context cues in pattern recognition, they overcome some of the other difficulties that have beset template and prototype theories. Feature theories propose that the recognition of objects occur, not by the matching of templates or prototypes, but through a process termed *feature analysis*. In this model stimuli are thought of as combinations of elemental features.

Let me try to explain how such a system works. If we consider how we discriminate between the capital letter 'A' and the capital letter 'H' I think you will get a better idea of what is meant by feature analysis. All letters are composed of a variety of lines. The lines are the elemental features of letters and may consist of vertical lines, horizontal lines, lines that join at roughly a forty-five degree angle and ones that are curved. Thus, the letter 'A' is represented by two lines forming a forty-five degree angle and joined together by a horizontal line at their mid-point. How the lines are combined to make the capital letter 'A' is thus specified. The letter 'H' is also composed of three straight lines but has only one feature in exact correspondence with the letter 'A', namely the horizontal line. In the case of the letter 'H' the horizontal line joins at their

5a *Seeing correctly and knowing what to do.*

mid-point two vertical lines and not ones that are sloping. This form of feature analysis allows for a greater flexibility in letter recognition than a template, since it extracts the essential features that define an 'A' as an 'A' and an 'H' as an 'H' and so on.

Similarly with Pippa. Her ability to recognize a kerb as a kerb, a door as a door and stairs as stairs is dependent upon a feature analysis which extracts their essential features. Indeed, there is physiological evidence from the brilliant work of David Hubel and Torsten Wiesel (1962) that the nerve cells of the primary visual cortex extract such features as horizontal and vertical lines and those at specific angles to the vertical. Take a look at photograph 5a in which a guide dog has evidently extracted the essential features of an A-frame on an obstacle course and has chosen correctly to go round rather than under it. Clearly a system which is designed to detect features rather than larger patterns will reduce the number of templates needed. In a feature analysis model of pattern recognition it is unnecessary to have a template for each pattern but only for each feature. Since similar features occur within many different patterns there is a considerable saving. Nevertheless, if the dog fails to discriminate accurately between different but similar stimuli containing common features, mistakes will be made. I have noticed how sometimes it is difficult for Pippa to know where the door is on the outside of a building when the adjoining windows are of a similar design and height to the door. In general, however, the ability of the dog to discriminate between similar but different stimulus objects is remarkable. For example, there never seems to be any difficulty for the guide dog in distinguishing between a kerb for a road (even if it has been lowered for wheelchair users) and a slope in the pavement for a driveway entrance to a house. Thankfully this is so as it would be a very slow journey if the guide dog stopped at every driveway with a down-slope or shallow kerb.

What seems to be happening in perception is that the dog is

extracting features from stimulus objects and combining them in the mind to form meaningful and recognizable patterns of those objects. Pattern recognition is thus dependent upon *feature extraction* and *feature combination.* With familiarity the dog will recognize stimulus objects without having to deliberately attend to them. It is when an object is unusual or unexpected that confusion and possible conflict of how to behave in its presence occurs. Nevertheless, the dog will attend to unfamiliar or unexpected stimulus events in order to make sense of what it sees or hears. It too will make an *effort after meaning*.

5b *A brief glance is now sufficient.*

"I was very aware of your concern Pippa on our first trip to London when you saw a motorized luggage buggy and trailer snaking along the platform towards us. I guessed from your reaction you had never seen one before. Probably your concern was all the greater as I had dropped the handle to your harness and you were not in a position to get me out of its way. Also part of the problem was the context in which you met with this strange motorized vehicle for the first time. If your first sight of one had been on a road rather than on a railway platform you would have shown little anxiety or surprise. However, the next time you saw one you only seemed to give it a brief glance as it passed you by. No longer was its behaviour unusual to you (photograph 5b)."

We too find some objects or events difficult to fathom and are in consequence somewhat fearful of them. Computers, or even the telephone, are treated with great suspicion by some. Our response to objects in the world is dependent upon our ability to understand and predict their behaviour. Familiarity may breed contempt but it also allows us to make accurate predictions about how people and objects are likely to behave. Frequently our fears are related to the manner in which we construct and impose meaning on the world of objects and people. And so it is for the dog. How the pup and young dog are introduced to a world of cars, children, trains, umbrellas and the like, will be important for how they respond to them in the future. Perception is an active process and one that also frequently involves our emotions – and in that respect we and the dog are quite unlike any computerized vision system. Neither the dog nor ourselves are passive recipients of environmental data. Both of us impose meaning on the world we see and hear as a consequence of past experience. For example, only when you have a knowledge of the braille code (stored within the connections of your brain) would you be able to perceive the dots on a braille display as a meaningful pattern.

"Similarly for you too Pippa. Only when you have had some experience with cars and bikes or with kerbs and ladders will you come to see them differently and know how to behave when you meet with them in a variety of situations."

As with template-matching and prototype theories, feature theories understate the role played by contextual cues and expectations in pattern recognition. Evidently pattern recognition is concerned with more than just feature extraction, feature combination and comparison with a stored mental prototype or template. To put it another way, we can say the recognition of objects for what they are is more than the result of *bottom-up processing*. Bottom-up processing involves the manner in which the features of stimulus objects are detected and then combined such that they can be identified with stored patterns. The process is called bottom-up because perception is built up from the little perceptual features of objects into larger units. But it would be impossible for me to read braille, for you to read a book or for the guide dog to recognize the 'kerbiness' of kerbs if perception were totally bottom-up. As an example, if we assume a letter is composed of five features, then the reading of this page of text would involve something in the order of fifteen thousand feature detections – between one hundred and three hundred feature detections per second depending upon the reading speed of the reader. Our minds could not work that fast. As you are aware, we do not need to detect each and every feature of a letter and we do not even have to read every word within a sentence to make sense of what we are reading. As was noted earlier, we can understand the meaning of sentences even though some letters of a word are replaced by an 'x'. For the guide dog too, context and partial appearance of objects allow for correct recognition without the need to detect every feature of an object. Such a detailed level of processing for object recognition would be quite prohibitive for the guide dog as it goes about the task of correctly 'reading' stimuli within the environment through which it has to guide. It just would not have enough time to identify objects in that way.

When context, expectations and past experience guide perception it is termed *top-down processing* of the information. It is the knowledge within Pippa's head that allows her to make the correct interpretations of the low level bottom-up data. Perception for the guide dog, as for ourselves, is the result of an interaction between bottom-up and top-down processing. Within a familiar context the dog will need to extract less information from the object in order to identify it for what it is. The guide dog certainly has to decide what is in its path in order that it can respond appropriately. Such pattern recognition would be extremely difficult, if not impossible, without some form of top-down processing.

This point can be made even more clearly by briefly examining face recognition. Recognition of faces is a high-level top-down process. Neither the dog nor ourselves carry out an exhaustive feature analysis of a person's face in order to recognize who it is.

Only a few days ago I opened the back-door to let the dogs in after their early morning trip outside. It is something my wife usually does, but on this particular morning she was elsewhere when the dogs barked to come back inside. Some repairs were being carried out to the house so I quickly grabbed the nearest dressing-gown to make myself decent before going through the kitchen to the rear door. It was my wife's full length dressing-gown I had put on. Pippa brushed by me as she came through the door. Then she took a second look to discover it was my head and face sticking out of the top of the very familiar dressing-gown. She leapt at me with pleasure once she had recognized who it was. Face recognition seems to be dependent upon the activity of specialized cells within the temporal lobe of the brain. At least we know this is so in people and monkeys. Occasionally damage to a person's brain following a stroke or viral infection has knocked out these face-recognition cells rendering the person unable to recognize the most familiar of faces, not even a photograph of the person sitting in front of them or their own face reflected in a mirror. In this condition which is called *prosopagnosia,* despite the fact the features of the face can be described perfectly, the face itself cannot be identified.

I mention these cases and the story of Pippa and the dressing-gown to demonstrate again what a complex process perception is in ourselves and animals. If perception were merely the product of bottom-up processing (sometimes called *data driven processing*) the animal would be broadly under the control of the environment. That is the way the behaviourists conceived of animal behaviour with the organism passively and automatically reacting to environmental stimuli. The use of top-down information, such as context and acquired knowledge, enables the organism to employ its past experience and conceptual structures to help it decide 'what is out there' and in turn guide its behaviour. Without this top-down processing system (sometimes called *concept driven processing*) pattern recognition at speed and whilst on the move would be extremely difficult for the guide dog. In a pure bottom-up system the amount of processing required would be overwhelming. Additionally, since the data from the environment is often unreliable it is important top-down processes impose meaning and significance on the data. It is because it is a conceptually driven process (in ourselves and the guide dog too) that perception itself has been claimed to be an act of considerable intelligence. That is not to say that bottom-up processing is not important. It is just that if the dog only processed data in a bottom-up manner the amount of data to be processed would be unbearable. Obviously, neither can perception simply be top-down. If that were the case, with no account being given to the incoming data', the dog and ourselves would operate in a world of pure fantasy.

Top-down knowledge is also of critical importance in the

process of selective attention by the guide dog. It is essential in helping the guide dog know to which aspects of the environment it should attend. Attention itself is a limited resource and the dog cannot process all the environmental data arriving at its sense organs. It needs to be selective as to which aspects of an ever changing environment it should attend. When too much information exists to be processed rapidly then attention is directed towards those features within the environment that are significant to the task in hand. At times the dog's attention will need to be focussed upon the position and direction of movement of cars, at others on the location of stairs and doors. Top-down processing in the form of context cues, conceptual knowledge and past experience enables the dog to selectively attend to task-significant events.

"Find the door Pippa. Clever girl. You make it seem so straightforward, but for you to recognize correctly the pattern of objects is not as simple as at first it might appear."

CHAPTER SIX
Thoughtful and Planned Behaviour

It was considered until quite recently that animal behaviour was best (and most scientifically) explained in observable stimulus-response terms. As we saw in chapter two, the efforts of behaviourism to rid animal psychology, and to some degree human psychology, of mentalistic explanations of behaviour resulted in the establishment of a *mechanistic* approach into the mainstream of psychology. The incremental (step-by-step) nature of learning stressed by the stimulus-response theorists, failed to account for the rapid *insightful* reasoning and flexible behaviour displayed by many animals. Animal behaviour is not as rigid as stimulus-response theory would have us believe.

Figure 6 illustrates the situation faced by Pippa and I on our way to work. Pippa had always turned right on the up-kerb of the pelican crossing and then sat at the down-kerb of the side road to my place of work. Since there was no pavement on the left-hand side of this road we always crossed to the other side and turned left on the up-kerb. But as you can see from the sketch, the pavement was up for repairs to the right of the crossing. If Pippa had turned to her right she would have had to treat the repairs as an off-kerb obstacle and also cross the side road. However, no such dangerous manoeuvre for Pippa! She had obviously weighed up the situation and without hesitation (and very much to my surprise) walked straight ahead and then veered to her right to join the side road further down, avoiding the dangerous main road altogether.

"Good thinking Pippa. You looked ahead and planned the neatest and safest way to achieve your goal of getting us both to the

pavement on the far side of the side road. Tolman would have enjoyed watching your insightful performance since he had always argued if anything remained fixed it was the goal to be achieved and not the individual behavioural responses."

In this naturally occuring 'detour problem', Pippa had to jiggle around the knowledge and action schemas within her brain in order that she could reach her goal. When Pippa consciously decides upon an alternative course of action in this way, she must continue to operate within a set of

FIGURE 6 *An insightful detour.*

'safety rules' – return to the pavement as soon as it is safe to do so, do not cross the road diagonally and so on. It is these mental representations, which intervene between the reception of sense data and a response, that enable Pippa and other animals to form and follow through plans for the attainment of their goals.

Those of you who are somewhat sceptical of the notion of animals acting purposively to a *plan*, should note ethologists like Griffin suggest the behaviour of many mammals may be directed by plans or strategies which are guided by the idea of a goal. The guide dog has to operate to a plan which is associated with a set of short range goals if safe and fluent mobility is to be achieved. An approach that suggests the actions of the guide dog are guided by a series of plans and a set of associated short range goals is significantly different from any stimulus-response explanation.

Although originally constructed to explain human performance, the seminal work of George Miller, Eugene Gallanter and Karl Pribram (1960) 'Plans and the Structure of Behaviour', is extremely useful for our understanding of skilled action by the guide dog. These authors proposed, as an alternative to the S-R reflex as the primary unit of behavioural analysis, the TOTE unit. TOTE stands for Test-Operate-Test-Exit.

Such a unit represents a two phase cyclical control process. The first phase of the sequence is the *test* phase which checks for any mismatch between the *actual* and *intended* state of affairs. The *operate* phase is set into action if the test phase detects a mismatch. Another *test* is then made and if incongruity still exists the *operate* phase is initiated again. The test-operate cycle is repeated until no mismatch is detected between the actual and intended state of affairs. Once the test phase detects no discrepancy between the intended and current position, the cycle is ended-*exit*.

It is during the test phase that the dog will need to check the current situation with the intended outcomes. This implies the dog does have a mental representation and a plan of action in respect of particular manoeuvres. Thus the dog's behaviour is orientated towards a goal, whether it be obstacle avoidance, road crossing or turning right or left to a command or guiding instruction.

The dog will have gained from its training an appreciation of what is intended in a particular situation or when a command or guiding instruction is given. Furthermore, if the dog is to be a *problem solver* it will need to have in its head an idea of what goals it has to achieve and an acceptable and safe plan for their accomplishment. Some examples will help to demonstrate the value of the TOTE model for the understanding of skilled action by the guide dog.

Consider first the dog guiding along a straight stretch of pavement where a lamp post and approaching pedestrian have to be avoided (figure 7). The TOTE sequence would be something like the following, where words are used to describe the representational and thought processes taking place within the mind of the guide dog.

FIGURE 7 *Avoiding pavement obstacles.*

Test – will the right hand side of the team miss the post?

Test answer – no.

Operate – move over left.

Test – will the right hand side of the team miss the post?

Test answer – yes.

Exit cycle.

Test – will the pedestrian be avoided?

Test answer – no.

Operate – move in right.

Test – will the pedestrian be avoided?

Test answer – yes.

Exit cycle.

Test – is the position on the pavement correct?

Test answer – no (too near edge).

Operate – move over left.

Test – is the position on the pavement correct?

Test answer – yes.

Exit cycle.

This relatively simple example illustrates the continual cycle of checks the dog has to make as it moves along a pavement. It has to *operate* following the *test* phase to ensure no mismatch exists between the *intended* and *actual* state of affairs. Thus, the TOTE unit permits the incorporation of planning, testing, matching, decision making and action processes into the structure of guide dog behaviour. A far more complete and satisfying account than that offered by stimulus-response theory.

A further advantage of the TOTE unit is that the *operate* phase can be expanded hierarchically to include any number of subordinate TOTE units. In the example figure 7, sub-routines could have been initiated as necessary following the *test* phase. If the pedestrian had quickly moved to his or her left, the dog would have been forced to stop or move to its left if there was space to do so. The dog, therefore, is having to continuously cycle through TOTE sequences.

The value of the TOTE unit for the analysis of skilled performance is revealed further in those situations where the guide dog has *advance information* of what it is expected to do. The most straight forward example of this, is when guiding along a pavement, as illustrated in the previous example. Here the dog's behaviour is orientated towards a future goal, rather than being controlled entirely by current or past stimulus events.

It cannot be assumed, however, that the dog will be provided, in all circumstances, with advance information. This is a critical issue for training, for if a rigid 'carrot and stick' (S-R) approach is employed, the dog may be given little opportunity to plan, think and test its way through the guiding work. A rule for training could be, 'wherever possible, provide the dog with advance information about what it is expected to do'.

The importance of advance information is apparent in the following example. Imagine the situation as illustrated in figure 8. I wished to turn left down the side road, having approached the junction with the main road on my right. I could have given

Pippa the guiding instruction "find left" a few yards before we reached the turn, but on this occasion I have let her go up to the kerb edge of the junction. Now a left-turn-behind is called for as a left-turn-in-front would place me in the road. Having stepped back a pace, the right thigh is slapped and the command "left" is given. Pippa will move to her right through roughly 270 degrees. Note that Pippa is given advance information as to where we are going, and although always moving to her right, she finally goes left in relation to her original position. If this example is repeated using the old combination turn (which is no longer taught), Pippa is given no advance information about the fact that we will eventually turn left.

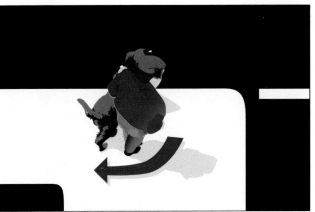

FIGURE 8 *Left-turn-behind.*

In the combination turn as illustrated in figure 9 the initial command is "back", and only when Pippa has turned through 180 degrees is the "right" command given. Not surprisingly, dogs find little difficulty with the left-turn-behind, where greater fluency is achieved. Furthermore, if the path to the left is temporarily blocked by pedestrians as illustrated in figure 10, Pippa will remain sitting until the route is clear. The TOTE sequence for the example in figure 10 is as follows.

Command – "left".

Test – is the pavement clear immediately left?

Test answer – no.

Operate – remain sitting (a decision is made.) (No exit from the cycle as the command "left" still stands.)

Test – is the pavement clear immediately left?

Test answer – yes.

Operate – move through 180 degrees.

FIGURE 9 *Old combination turn.*

Test – is the pavement clear to the right?

Test answer – yes.

Operate – move through a further 90 degrees.

Test – turn completed?

Test answer – yes.

Exit cycle.

Test – central pavement position?

Test answer – yes.

Exit cycle.

As feedback loops are thought to operate between the *test* and *operate* phases, the dog's behaviour is relatively flexible and responsive to environmental changes. That is to say, the dog can change its behaviour quickly in accord with environmental demands. Provided the dog appreciates what it is trying to achieve, within certain 'safety rules', it can adapt its behaviour to attain the prescribed goals. Furthermore, if the dog is on a familiar route, such as going home from work, then its plan of action is not simply concerned with straight forward obstacle avoidance,

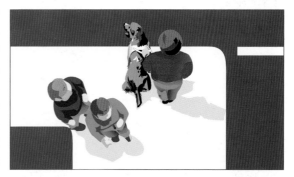

FIGURE 10 Waiting until the pavement is clear.

but more long-range. Road crossings, turns and so forth, become sub-routines of the longer range plan. To put it another way, the guide dog is capable of appreciating in broad terms the task which has to be achieved and the behaviours necessary for attainment of the goal. That is why Pippa was able to make that insightful detour on our way to work. It was a very reasonable deduction of hers that once we had decided to cross the road my intended destination was my place of work – it was a route we had taken many times before!

Since the guide dog, when on a familiar route, can usually deduce the overall goal of the journey, it is helpful to allow the dog to choose at which point to cross the road, so that blocked pavements, road works and parked cars can be avoided. The dog is being given the valuable opportunity to *take charge* in a situation in which it knows where it is going and what it has to do. In short its actions are purposive and guided by a plan.

CHAPTER SEVEN
A Skilful Animal

Problem solving and planned behaviour by animals and ourselves suggests we both have a level of consciousness that allows us to appreciate we prefer some states of affairs in the world rather than others and an ability to achieve them through our own actions. But I must take care not to foster the idea only people and highly intelligent animals with evident planning and problem solving skills are consciously aware of what they are doing. Even the humble chicken may 'decide' to cross the road because it 'believes' it will be 'happier' on the other side! No, many other animals would seem capable of acting consciously to achieve their goals. It is just that much easier to observe *consciousness at work* when people and 'intelligent' animals are problem solving – perhaps making an 'insightful' detour to avoid a pavement obstacle without going into a busy main road.

However, we do many things without being consciously aware of what we are doing. In fact, neither we nor animals are conscious of most of the cognitive activities taking place within our brains. As an example, we are not aware of the processes involved in pattern recognition. The way in which salient features of an object are extracted and combined to facilitate the identification of stimuli operate outside conscious awareness. All we are aware of is the visual, sound or tactile image. What we experience is the sight of a yellow labrador (which we may recognize as one belonging to a friend or neighbour), the sound pattern of our own name (and usually who is calling us) or the immediate tactile recognition it is a pound coin we have taken out of our purse or pocket. When I ask Pippa to "sit", "stay" or "come", she is obviously not aware of the cognitive processes involved in the recognition of these meaningful sound patterns, only of the sound patterns themselves and who is giving the command.

Apparently, many mental activities involved in our own and the dog's cognition are not carried out consciously. This is also true of skilled action. Although we may talk of some complex (and largely innate) behaviours displayed by animals as *skilful*, psychology has generally reserved the term *skill* for those intricate patterns of behaviour acquired by people as a result of practice.

> *"But Pippa, you have learned to be skilful too. You show in so many aspects of your work you are not only a conscious animal, but also a skilful one. Thinking of* **you** *as 'skilful' will help me and others to understand more clearly how you have learned to be such a confident and fluent guide. And, as with skilful people, to perform skilfully does not mean you have to be consciously aware of everything you are doing all of the time."*

An experienced motorist can be mentally miles away and still drive fluently. We find the timing in the tennis stroke can be lost and the concert pianist caused to stumble over the keys, when the player in either case thinks too much about what he or she is doing.

Consider for a moment the processes involved in skill learning by the guide dog and car driver. They both need to pay conscious attention to the component elements of the skilled activity during the early period of instruction. Just as the learner driver has to check deliberately each step in a series of required actions – depress the clutch, engage first gear, release the hand-brake – so Pippa, during the early period of her training, had to turn her head to check she was correctly positioned to successfully avoid scaffolding or a telegraph pole.

Even today, now she is an experienced guide, Pippa still checks to make sure I am safe when guiding through the tightest of spaces. In photograph 7a she glances back to ensure the steel hawser and telegraph pole are cleared. Just to show how skilful she can be, Pippa expertly manoeuvres me around the same pavement obstacle in the opposite direction (photograph 7b). A characteristic of skill learning is that after some period of extended practice, many of the individual behavioural components of the skill become inaccessible to conscious awareness. As we have just seen, trying to bring them to the conscious level can interfere with the efficiency of the performance. Highly skilled behaviour frequently requires little conscious attention, until, of course, the unexpected happens. Consciousness comes back into its own when having to deal with a novel or unexpected event.

7a *Just checking.*

> *"Well done Pippa. It must have been difficult for you to anticipate the car was about to turn across in front of us."*

The components of well practiced motor behaviours are down-graded. They are pushed out of the forefront of consciousness and so require less attentional focus for their execution as

7b *What a skilful piece of work!*

they become *automatic* and less *deliberate*. As skill learning by the dog progresses, we may hypothesize that conscious control shifts away from the smaller elements of the task to concerns about higher order cognitive activities such as decision making and planning. Most of the fine grain aspects of the movement skills are taken over by lower centres in the central nervous system.

An analogy that should help us to appreciate the hierarchical nature of skilled action is offered by Fitts and Posner (1967). They ask us to imagine a company president issuing a command that is then organized and executed by progressively lower levels of the company work-force, without the president having to worry about the details of the job. The decision making and planning activities taking place within the brain can be equated with the company president's decision making and planning function. Evidently, motor skills possessed by ourselves and the guide dog too, have a higher level cognitive component which is fundamental for their execution. The higher level cognitive activities of decision making and planning are essential in the generation and control of all skilled motor behaviours. Just about all motor behaviours are under cognitive control even though the movements of the skill are eventually carried out relatively automatically.

Attention is a limited cognitive resource and the process of down-grading prevents, or at least reduces, the possibility of subjecting the dog to a state of *information overload* when it is having to cope with difficult or novel situations. The same problem is faced by the car driver. If bombarded with just too much visual and auditory data, the driving skill will break down. It is difficult for the inexperienced driver or guide dog to know what events should be attended to and there seems to be far too little time available to take the decisions which are necessary. Errors will be made and the driver and guide dog alike are likely to become stressed. The stress will in turn depress further their ability to effectively process information and make correct guiding or driving decisions. Fortunately, experience will give the dog knowledge of which events in a particular situation need to be attended to and which may be safely ignored. Filtering out superfluous information from the environment is necessary for the production of skilful guiding behaviours.

If the guide dog is to be able to disentangle and make sense of the vast amount of incoming data from the environment it will need also to develop a means of organizing the relevant perceptual information that is pertinent to the task. Guide dog skills require the perception and interpretation of specific features of the environment; kerbs, street furniture and the approach of pedestrian and vehicle traffic. Following the analysis of such perceptual data, the guide dog has to make an appropriate response. Although both perceiving and responding call for a high level of skilfulness from the guide dog, it is at the sensory or input end of the dog's cognitive system that the information processing demand is greatest.

Bartlett (1943) and Alan Welford (1976) both argue the most important of the processes underlying the acquisition of motor skills is on the input side of the task. For effective guiding actions the guide dog will need to develop a system of *perceptual organization* which filters and orders the incoming stimuli so as to maximize the value of the information that can be handled by its limited information processing system. As the guide dog gains experience about the task, much of the information coming in through its sense organs (visual, auditory, olfactory and tactile) becomes redundant. That is to say, many of the events in the environment have to be recognized as unimportant to the task. In this regard, certain distracting behaviours, such as sniffing and dog-watching, need to be checked as they can seriously interfere with the processing of task-relevant information. They are very much 'no no' behaviours for the guide dog when at work.

Further redundancy of information from the environment may be achieved in those situations where the guide dog can learn that a series of signals appear in a relatively fixed order. For example, only the 's' of the command 'sit' has to be pronounced for the command to be obeyed by the experienced guide dog, particularly if the context cues are supportive of the action. Similarly with other commands, guiding instructions and cues, only the initial part of the word or action is required for the dog to be able to predict the remaining signals. Even the instructor spelling out to the student under training, the 'f-o-r' of the 'forward' command is sufficient information for some dogs to leave the down-kerb. In these examples the necessary information is contained within the first part of a word or action, the remainder being redundant.

However, in relation to the guiding task itself, the occurrence of unchanging sequences of events is rare. The dog when guiding is on the move, and even the position of stationary objects such as lamp posts have to be judged against the relative position of pedestrian traffic, prams and street furniture. The guide dog's environment is usually continuously changing. In such situations the sequence of environmental signals is clearly not invariant. Nevertheless, the guide dog will need to develop a perceptual organization which renders a high percentage of the visual, auditory, olfactory and tactile information redundant, if *information overload* is to be avoided. The dog has to attend to the genuinely useful cues which indicate what action is needed to ensure progressive and safe mobility.

Greater efficiency in processing the sensory input is dependent upon the dog developing a set of probabilities about the sequence of signals from the environment. Rather than operating on an invariant order of signals, an appreciation needs to be acquired by the dog that one signal is more likely to be followed by a particular series of signals rather than another. The identification of *task specific* cues within a *framework of probabilities* will provide the dog with advanced warning of changing conditions. The experienced guide dog when working in a busy pedestrian precinct will be capable of looking ahead and predicting where gaps in the crowd are most likely to occur (photograph 7c).

Anticipation of this type is dependent upon the |dog *understanding* what the task entails and identifying those cues which will ensure effective progress. Greater efficiency in processing the sensory input will be most successfully achieved if the dog is supported to use its own initiative to *think* its way through the work.

The concept of *chunking* is also useful in helping us understand how fluent guiding behaviour is gradually achieved by the guide dog. Chunking is of two types: one is concerned with the sensory end of the processing system, *input chunking*, and the other with the effector or motor end, *output chunking*.

7c *Spotting the gap.*

Input chunking is the means whereby a series of stimuli or events are grouped together as a whole or pattern such that they are processed as a single unit of information. Chunking information in this way is dependent upon the dog *looking ahead*. To explain this important processing function further,

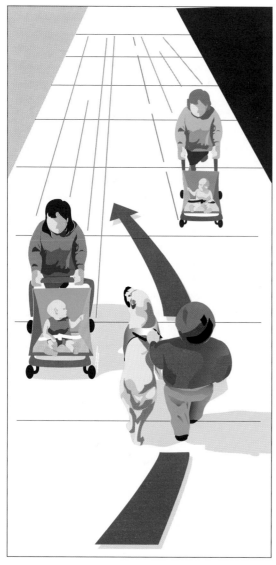

FIGURE 11 *Planning ahead.*

imagine two prams, some thirty yards ahead, are approaching the guide dog team as illustrated in figure 11. If pram A (which is to the left side of the pavement as viewed from the team's position) is travelling faster than pram B, the dog will need first to move to its right to avoid pram A, and then quickly move to the left to avoid pram B and slide through the gap. Clearly, the dog has to look well ahead and plan its actions in advance. It can of course, only work on probabilities of occurrence and not on certainties. Pram B, for example, might at the last moment veer to its right. The dog would then have to move quickly to its right or stop if a collision was to be avoided.

One of the significant differences between the novice and skilled guide dog is to be seen in the experienced dog's ability to *look ahead* and *chunk* the information.

It is very evident that the experienced guide dog, as with the expert motorist, is not responding to discrete stimuli one after another. Let me try and clarify this point further. Imagine a busy town centre street with a variety of vehicles moving in different directions and at different speeds confronting the guide dog team about to cross the road. There may be a number of obstructions that prevent a clear view of the road, such as stationary vehicles, road works, street furniture, pedestrians and prams. The kerb edge may be easily distinguished by a drop of several inches, it might have been lowered to allow for wheelchairs and prams or it may be signalled only by a yellow line or a change in material. Distinguishing the boundary between road and pavement may be a far from trivial task, especially when streets may be designated 'pedestrian only' at certain times of the day.

It is clear from this description there are a considerable number of possible combinations of stimulus events or variables which confront the guide dog about to cross the road. Which cues should be attended to? Which cues are redundant or irrelevant? Which set of conditions is necessary to permit a safe crossing of the road? If the dog had to discriminate the presence or absence of any one of this set of variables and then cross-match each with every other variable, its processing system would soon be overloaded with information which it just could not handle in the time available.

When a discrimination is made between the presence or absence of a stimulus, as when distinguishing whether a light is on or off, we say the animal has made a *binary distinction*. Let us suppose that in road crossing the dog has to make a binary distinction in regard to the presence or absence of ten relevant events or variables, and in turn cross-match each with one another. In this case there are potentially 1,024 (2^{10}) combinations of these ten events which are possible. Adding a further factor doubles the number of possible combinations, and this does not take account of the fact that some stimulus events which have to be discriminated are continuous rather than binary; for example, the distance of an oncoming vehicle as opposed to the presence or absence of a stationary vehicle.

If the guide dog's responses are determined by combinations of these stimuli, then it would have to learn a suitable response to an enormous number of stimulus combinations. But it cannot really be like that at all. Since the guide dog can take a number of factors into account at the same time when crossing roads, such as the position, speed and direction of vehicle traffic, it must have some mental mechanism which enables it to overcome, what has been called, the *combinatorial explosion*. That is to say, it will need to have an effective way of dealing with a variety of related and significant events quickly and accurately. How is this achieved? The incoming data is *filtered, chunked, organized, classified* and assigned meaning by interactive processing with mental schemata, which define the *what* and the *how* of the guiding task. These interrelated cognitive activities taking place within the guide dog's brain, enable it to cope efficiently with a wide range of difficult and ever-changing environments with speed and accuracy.

And to complete the picture, chunking on the output side is concerned with the grouping of movement sequences. Motor fluency is brought about by two operations. Firstly, separate actions are integrated together into a single *chunk* which is then run off as a single unit of behaviour. Secondly, the guide dog gradually develops the capability to overlap in time a sequence of movements with another. That is to say, preparation (and even movement itself) for one series of actions is commenced before a previous sequence of actions has been completed.

Greater efficiency on the input side will result in improved output efficiency. The latter is dependent, at least to some degree, on the former. Practice provides the opportunity for *fine tuning* both input and output systems. Skill learning is a gradual process, but eventually the guide dog is able to cope with some very difficult situations confidently and fluently without undue stress.

CHAPTER EIGHT

The Translation of Knowledge into Action

Pippa moves to the corner of the field and zig-zags her way back towards me as she searches systematically for her ball (photograph 8a). She has registered in her mind (within the connections of her brain) a clear conceptual representation of what constitutes the characteristics of a ball, and more importantly for her, the particular features of her own rubber ball. It is also evident Pippa has developed the concept of *object permanence.* For her, unlike a one month old child, out of sight does not mean out of mind! Pippa knows the ball has to be found somewhere.

8a *Out of sight does not mean out of mind.*

Through her observations and actions on the world she has acquired a knowledge of the physical and behavioural characteristics of many objects. She can impose meaning on what she sees and hears. As we saw in chapter five, perception is the result of the interaction of *bottom-up* and *top-down* processing. Pippa's top-down knowledge means she knows exactly what to do when her collar or harness is presented to her in a particular fashion. She puts her head through them both as she recognizes these things for what they are.

"We have noted already Pippa, your ability to discriminate between ladders and scaffolding, cars and people and your understanding of what to do when you meet with them. However, it is not just objects you have to recognize. You also have to deal with complex stimulus event relationships. For example, before leaving the down-kerb of a road you must first ensure (with support from me) all the conditions for a safe road crossing are satisfied."

Have a look at the photographs in the series 8b through to 8d. They should give you a good idea of what a difficult job safe road crossing is for the guide dog. In the first of the series (8b) Pippa has decided correctly not to leave the down-kerb. She has

8b *Wait.*

realized (by first listening and then checking by looking) a car is about to turn off the main road and pass in front of us. Fortunately, Pippa does not wait for all vehicles travelling on the main road – that would make for very slow progress. She waits only for the traffic which she anticipates may turn off the main road by a change in their engine noise, speed and position. There are many cues to which the guide dog should attend if safe road crossing is to be achieved.

"Well done Pippa. You have gradually acquired an appreciation of the task significant cues to which you should attend if you are going to be in a position to predict the possible course of events."

8c *A wise decision.*

As can be seen in photograph 8c, Pippa has again made the wise decision to remain sitting at the kerb edge, as the far traffic approaching the junction from the left is too near and travelling too fast to permit a safe road crossing.

8d *Safe to cross.*

On most roads of this width I have not encouraged her to leave the down-kerb and stop in the middle of the road for approaching far traffic. On relatively narrow roads I feel much happier if the road is clear in both directions before we cross. However, as soon as the road is clear, Pippa must move off immediately. She needs to appreciate a clear road is one that can be safely crossed. In photograph 8d you can see Pippa has started to move off from the down kerb as the car at the junction begins to pull away. She (and I) will have checked that no further vehicle is approaching the junction from the left and nothing is about to turn across in front of us from the right. The position, direction and speed of traffic must all be taken into account in this most taxing of guide dog skills. Safe road crossing is dependent upon the dog thinking about what it is doing.

Perhaps the capacity for mental representation, and in turn thought, emerged out of the necessity of animals to find their way around in the world. The need for effective navigation may have been crucial in the evolution of thought in animals as well as in ourselves. Two cognitive capacities would seem to be necessary for effective and purposeful navigation by animals. Firstly, a capacity to represent a model of the outside world inside their heads, and secondly, a capacity for thought to guide their actions in the world.

The guide dog must possess these two cognitive attributes if effective performance is to be achieved. We can confidently infer from observations of Pippa's skilful behaviour that she has the capacity to represent and manipulate knowledge about the world in general and that related to her guiding work in particular. For the guide dog to use thought to guide its actions, first it will need to know *what* it has to do in a particular situation, for example, when meeting with ladders, approaching kerbs or crossing roads. Mental representations that are concerned with event relationships form part of what has been called the animal's *declarative knowledge system*. Such knowledge about the world is thought to be stored within the memory system in the form of a proposition which states the relationship between events. Pippa's declarative knowledge system contains 'statements' about how she should behave when guiding:

Stop and sit at all road kerbs.

Do not leave the down-kerb if a car is close and approaching on the near side of the road.

All roads must be crossed in a straight-line in order to hit the up-kerb.

All ladders must be negotiated by going round rather than under them.

It is called the declarative knowledge system because it contains declarative 'statements' about *what* to do in a particular situation. We humans develop our declarative knowledge systems by reading, listening to instructions, observation and demonstration. In fact, much of our knowledge of *what* to do is contained in the form of a verbal statement – depress the clutch before engaging first gear. Although there is some evidence animals may acquire behaviours by means of observational learning, note the value of running a young dog with an older and more experienced one when sheep trialling, in the main, the guide dog acquires its declarative knowledge by *doing*. Even if this is not as true for the human operator, it is not clear to what extent skilled motor learning could develop without any actual movement by the operator. One example is learning to drive a car. As I am sure you will appreciate, there is a world of difference between knowing *what* is required in changing gear and actually being able to *do* it fluently. Albert Bandura (1986) summarized this point by quipping,

A novice given complete information on how to ski, a set of decision rules, and then launched from a mountain top would most likely end up in an orthopedic ward.

In order for the guide dog to be skilful it must translate declarative knowledge into action, known as *procedural knowledge*. Procedural knowledge is concerned with knowing *how* to do something as opposed to declarative knowledge which is concerned with knowing *what* to do. The distinction is a valuable one for the understanding of skill learning by the guide dog. Skilful behaviour is dependent upon the guide dog knowing both *what* it has to do and *how* to do it. We too have developed many *facts* about events in the world. The information we have acquired and stored in our declarative knowledge systems allows us to make predictions about what is likely to happen next in a particular situation.

Our knowledge about objects and event relationships provides a framework that enables us to make sense of what we see and hear and in turn helps to guide our actions in the world. Just reflect upon how difficult it would be for you to cross a busy street safely without knowledge of how traffic on the highway behaves. You would be in a similar position to a very young child or perhaps even a man from Mars. We have learned to recognize objects and appreciate what cues are of particular significance to us in a wide range of situations. It is those stored facts about the world with which we think. We use thought in order to know *how* to act to attain specified ends, that is procedural knowledge, and the same is true for the guide dog. It too will need to know *how* to act to achieve set goals. Therefore, a key feature of motor skill learning for the guide dog is the means by which knowledge about the guiding task is translated into effective action. The mental model of the guiding task which the guide dog holds within its declarative and procedural knowledge systems is the product of training and experience.

The procedural knowledge system may be thought of as a set of rules which acts with the declarative knowledge system to ensure the dog's actions are correct for the situation. Therefore, the main function of the motor programme (which controls the dog's movements) is to provide connections between declarative knowledge (the *what* of the guiding task) and action (the *how* of the guiding task).

The TOTE cycle is another way of representing the point that effective performance by the guide dog is dependent upon it shuttling back and forth between its declarative and procedural knowledge systems. As it guides along a pavement it has continually to check whether there is any mismatch between the actual and intended state of affairs. It is also within the dog's declarative knowledge system that the goals the dog has to attain are stored. Using the language of the TOTE cycle (chapter six) we can say that if the dog detects a mismatch between the intended and actual state of affairs, the operate phase is set into action. Following the operate phase a further test is made and if incongruity still exists the operate phase is initiated again. It is during the test phase the dog will have to draw upon knowledge (about the task) from within its declarative knowledge system. Within the operate phase the procedural knowledge system comes into play.

"Yes Pippa, as you guide along a pavement you will need constantly to shuttle back and forth between your declarative and procedural knowledge systems to make sure there is no mismatch between the actual and intended state of affairs."

You may find it helpful if I use the example from chapter six (figure 7) where the dog is guiding along a pavement on which a lamp post has to be avoided. I will include in the sequence reference to the declarative and procedural memory systems of the dog.

Test – will the right-hand side of the team miss the post? (The dog has stored within its declarative memory the knowledge that posts have to be avoided.)

Test answer – no. (Something must be done to match the actual state of affairs with that which is intended.)

Operate – move over left. (The declarative and procedural systems operate together to achieve the intended outcome.)

Test – will the right-hand side of the team miss the post?

Test answer – yes. (The actual and intended state of affairs are satisfied.)

Exit cycle.

An example of the guide dog's traffic work should also help you to appreciate how important it is for the dog to know *what* it has to do when crossing roads. It needs to have a *real* understanding of what this part of its job is all about.

Consider the traffic situation presented to Pippa illustrated in photograph 8e. Apart from the situation when there is no traffic around at all, the photograph represents perhaps the most straight forward of traffic tasks for the guide dog. A vehicle is approaching the T-junction from the right on the near side of the road. Pippa has to weigh-up as she sits at the kerb edge:

(i)   The distance of the car from the crossing point.

(ii)   The direction in which the car is travelling – towards or away from the junction.

(iii) If the car is travelling towards the junction, its speed of approach.

(iv) On this narrow road, if the far lane is free of traffic.

And let me remind you once more, Pippa in this (and all other situations) must be aware of those aspects

8e *Look right.*

of the environment to which she should attend. The analysis demanded of Pippa in relation to the above situation may be represented as follows.

Test 1 – is traffic approaching from the right?

Test answer – Yes. (Will also need to estimate distance and speed of approach.)

Test 2 – is the far lane clear and likely to remain so? (The traffic identified in Test 1 makes Test 2 redundant but I get the impression Pippa takes account of both when approaching the kerb edge of the road.)

Test answer – yes.

Operate – remain sitting as the near traffic approaching from the right does not permit a safe road crossing.

Repeat Test 1 – is traffic approaching from the right?

Test answer – no.

Repeat Test 2 – is the far lane clear and likely to remain so?

Test answer – yes.

Operate – start to cross the road.

Test (while crossing) – is the far lane clear and going to remain so?

Test answer – yes.

Operate – continue to cross the road to the up-kerb.

Exit cycle.

We see in many aspects of the guide dog's work how with practice their performance becomes better integrated and coordinated. This greater fluency is the result of a speeding up of decision time. The experienced guide dog learns to respond to whole patterns rather than to individual components of a situation. The necessity for the guide dog to analyse the scene as a whole is particularly evident in regard to their traffic work. As we saw in the last chapter, without a perceptual system to organize the incoming data, the dog's processing system would become overloaded to such an extent it would be unable to cope with the *combinatorial explosion* presented by the 'traffic problem'.

I remember as a teenager my first experience of driving through London in the rush hour. I could not rely on other drivers to give me time as I struggled to read road signs. I had not yet developed a perceptual organization that could deal effectively with so much incoming information. My gear changing became jerky and my breaking too late and harsh. No longer did I seem to have time to look ahead and plan my actions – and then it began to rain! My harsh breaking on a greasy road caused me to skid. Although I had within my declarative knowledge system a statement which told me to steer into the skid, knowing *what* to do is not quite the same as knowing *how* to do it; especially in an emergency! I, like the youthful guide dog, was not yet able to effectively translate knowledge into action.

During the period of training when the guide dog is being shown *what* to do by use of the leash, hand movements and the voice, it may be thought of as operating within a declarative mode. The dog during the *showing* stage will probably move slowly, perhaps cautiously and without fluency. It is having to check continually what it is doing is correct. We too may have difficulty in retrieving 'instructions' from our memory store of what we should do next – depress the clutch, engage first gear – but what about checking the rear view mirror and gently pressing the accelerator?

Motor skill learning is the gradual shift from a declarative or showing mode to a procedural one. John Anderson would say, "Declarative knowledge gradually becomes proceduralized". The value of viewing guide dog learning in this way is the emphasis it places on the knowledge structures which support skilled performance. One of the most important functions of training is to provide the dog with the opportunity to develop an overall grasp of its guiding role. Although such *understanding* is difficult to describe in behavioural terms, it is broadly related to the confidence with which correct decisions are taken by the dog. As with human skilled operators, the guide dog too needs a knowledge system with which to direct and coordinate its actions.

Skilful behaviour by the guide dog *cannot* be explained away as the outcome of conditioning alone. Skill acquisition by the guide dog is dependent upon the development of a coherent network of mental representations. Following Kenneth Craik (1943) it would seem one of the main functions of brains (of animals and humans alike) is to provide an internal model of external reality. Critical for the guide dog's work is the internalisation of the objective external world in terms of an appreciation of the complex relationship between objects and actions. Skilful guiding behaviours could only emerge in an animal with the capacity for that mental activity we call *thought.*

CHAPTER NINE
The Confident Partnership

Despite an abundance of talent or knowledge, it is frequently the confidence we have in ourselves and in our own abilities that determines whether or not we are successful at what we are doing. Our confidence may be knocked by any one of a number of life experiences, but often our concerns are centred upon the negative outcomes we anticipate might be associated with our own actions. We may be fearful of anticipated failure, criticism or ridicule. Do you remember your last job interview or your first public talk? Many situations may be seen as potentially punishing for us, and when our expectations about outcomes are negative, the resulting emotion is one of fear or anxiety.

Whether our fears are real or imagined, our alarm reaction is triggered. Adrenalin is automatically secreted, the heart rate increases, muscles are tensed, jaws are clenched, as we prepare ourselves for fight or flight. It is a protective reaction that can so easily get out of hand and panic may result. High levels of anxious arousal can seriously affect the quality and nature of our thoughts and actions. A certain level of arousal is necessary for any form of mental or physical activity, but too much can be quite debilitating. High levels of anxiety limit our ability to process information from the environment and translate our thoughts into effective action. How poorly some of us have performed when taking a driving test, sitting an exam or delivering a lecture, but not because we did not know *what* to do or *how* to do it. Had we not in previous and more relaxed circumstances been able to perform quite competently? If only we could predict with confidence our actions would have a positive pay-off for us. Being able to predict that our actions are likely to produce positive outcomes allows us to perform with confidence.

And if I apply these same principles to skill acquisition by the guide dog, we will recognize the importance of a programme of education which is *positively* orientated. That is to say, one in which physical punishment is kept to an absolute minimum and the behaviours essential for guiding are gradually shaped-up through the consistent and judicious giving of positive reinforcers – mainly verbal and physical praise – for correct behaviour. The confident, relaxed and attentive guide is likely to be the dog that can predict its own actions will be broadly rewarding.

> *"Yes, it is the same for you Pippa as it is for me when coping with difficult and potentially frightening situations. You need to be sure the decisions you take are going to be supported by me. And when you make an occasional mistake I hope you are confident I will not come down on you like a ton of bricks. I guess over the years we have learned to predict each others behaviour pretty well. I know on some occasions you even seem able to read my mind."*

Proficient guide dog work is the product of a team effort. The gradual emergence of an effective team will be dependent upon both partners (dog and instructor or dog and guide dog owner) developing a confidence in themselves and in each other. In this area we see the complex and necessary interdependence within the training and guiding partnership of human and dog. The basic elements of this four-way interplay, usefully called the *confidence quadrangle* by T. Austin in 1978, is illustrated in figure 12.

Firstly, the dog has to develop a confidence in itself as a dog and in its ability to do the guiding work. The security provided by the mother, offering a buffer against environmental stress, the opportunities for playful exploration alongside its brothers

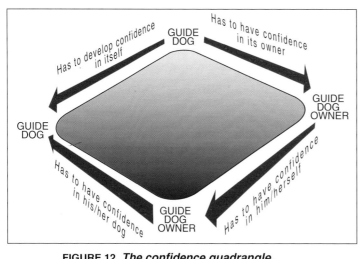

FIGURE 12 *The confidence quadrangle.*

and sisters, and the quality of the early attachments with humans are all likely to contribute to the young pup's confidence in itself. During the early puppy walking period the manner in which the dog is gradually introduced to a widening environment of people, animals, traffic and shops is fundamental to the young dog's understanding of itself and the world of which it is a part. Although temperamental variations will affect the dog's reactions to such events, the supportive and secure relationship it develops with the puppy walker (and their family) will be significant to the emergence of a confident dog.

Additionally, the consistency and timing with which positive reinforcers (and negative ones on some occasions) are delivered during early obedience training, will be significant. Confidence is most likely to develop in a relatively predictable world. The dog, even at this stage, must begin to learn about the consequences attached to its own actions. Consistency in the manner in which the dog is handled is a critical ingredient. Motivational and emotional problems could be the outcome for the dog that has been handled inconsistently. It is crucial to maintain the dog's enjoyment of learning. A positive, encouraging, consistent and playful approach would seem to be the best guarantee for the development of a confident and willing learner and worker.

As has been made clear, we may view the guide dog primarily as a decision maker. The quality of the decisions by the guide dog will be very dependent upon the confidence it has in its guiding role. *Purposeful* and *positive* decision making may only be acquired by the dog that is given the opportunity to *understand* the task and supported in the decisions it has to make. One of the main intentions of training is the development of a confident decision making guide dog. There are always dangers inherent in a training programme which over-uses punishment (particularly physical punishment) at any time, but especially during the early period of skill acquisition. When punishment is used inappropriately or inconsistently, the dog can so easily become overconcerned about an anticipated correction rather than attending to the task.

The concept of *learned helplessness*, first put forward by Seligman and his colleagues in the sixties, is useful to us here. They found that after dogs had been exposed to several trials of inescapable shock by being restrained in a harness, they failed to relearn the escape response once the harness had been removed. Indeed, relearning of the escape response only occurred after the dogs had been physically dragged away from the shock situation on a number of occasions. It seemed as if the dogs' natural escape response had been extinguished in the inescapable shock situation. They had come to *believe* they were unable to control environmental events through their own behaviour – they had learned to be *helpless.*

> *"Pippa, provided I remember you are a skilful animal with highly developed predictive skills, I know I will continue to be very careful when and where I use any form of physical punishment to change your behaviour. As with people when they are performing a skill, a physical correction is more likely to hinder rather than aid understanding, fluency or confidence in the task."*

One of the most gratifying features of a positively orientated training programme is the calm confidence with which the dogs approach their work. As the guide dog develops an understanding of the task, it should – if supported to do so –

have the confidence to overrule the guide dog owner or instructor. For example, leave the down-kerb with positive intent when it is clear to do so, despite the anxious hesitation of the guide dog owner, or keep straight on a road crossing even when the instructor is tempting it to go off-line.

In these, and many other examples from their work, the guide dog is being asked to *take charge.* This raises a further question in regard to training procedures, namely, in what situations should the dog be more dominant in relation to the handler, and when should it be relatively submissive? This presents a real difficulty, as with pet dogs and working dogs alike, dominance by the handler, as pack-leader, is seen by many as an essential ingredient of obedience and/or work training. The resolution of this dominance-submission conflict for guide dog training is critical since the dog, for the most part, is asked to take responsibility for the guiding decisions – the task is such that it could not be otherwise. Perhaps a partial solution to this training dilemma may be found in a questioning of some of the assumptions we hold about the necessity of human dominance for effective control of the dog. The deep attachment the dog has for its owner, and its nearly insatiable desire to please, means the need to resort to physical punishment to gain pack leadership for the purpose of behavioural control is unnecessary. In the wild it is not always the most dominant or strongest animal that is the accepted leader of the pack. Foresight and the possession of hunting, tracking and problem solving skills may be far more important in determining pack leadership. In regard to just about all cognitive activities, it is the human animal which holds all the aces. Physical punishment should be reserved for the genuinely important 'no no' behaviours for the guide dog when at work, such as sniffing, animal interest and ball watching. Even the basic behaviours of sitting, standing, staying and heeling can be most efficiently achieved by the giving of praise and perhaps a tit-bit during the early stages of learning.

The guide dog must, of course, be obedient and follow instructions, in and out of harness. Most importantly however, it needs to develop the confidence when at work to be *in charge* in many situations. Provided the decisions taken by the dog are supported, with a minimum level of interference, it will gradually develop an appreciation of those situations in which it is normally expected to assume responsibility.

Naturally the confidence the dog develops in itself is closely related to the confidence it has in its puppy walker, instructor and finally guide dog owner. This list of human attachment figures is the minimum number of people with whom the guide dog will be expected to relate during its upbringing and training. A change of person is usually accompanied by a change in environment – from the home of the puppy walker to the training centre and finally to the blind person's home and workplace. Surprisingly few of the dogs break down during these stressful upheavals. Many dogs however, do experience stress levels which affect their confidence and will to learn. Again the emotional and cognitive systems are seen to be closely entwined in their contribution to the dog's behaviour and performance. Despite the difficulties it is vital the dog's trust and confidence in its current handler are developed and maintained. In the final analysis it is the confidence the dog develops in its long-term partner which is most critical. The *quality* of the earlier attachments, the methods adopted during training and the temperament of the dog will all bear upon the ultimate confidence the dog will have in the guide dog owner.

Evidently, this second component of the *confidence quadrangle* – the confidence the dog has in its handler – is associated closely with the first component – the confidence the dog has in itself. A summary guideline for the successful development of both these aspects of the quadrangle might be, 'be consistent but flexible, positive but firm, confident but sensitive, supportive but aware and relaxed but attentive'.

The dog's willingness to work, learn and take decisions in

Glossary

ABILITY – a capacity or skill. May speak of innate (unlearned) or acquired (learned) abilities. *See also* SKILL.

ACHIEVEMENT – the successful reaching of a goal or sub-goal.

ACQUISITION – a particular skill, ability or level of competence gained by an animal or human.

ADAPTATION – the process by which an animal or human adjusts to an environment, so they may survive or benefit.

An animal or human may adapt:
> [i]   as a result of evolutionary processes through which the gene pool of the species as a whole is strengthened by the process of natural selection.
> [ii]   where an individual member of a species adapts to a specific environment by means of learning.

ADJUSTMENT – modifications in behaviour that enable an animal or human to adapt successfully to their environment.

ADVANCE INFORMATION – used specifically in the book to refer to guiding instructions given to the guide dog as far ahead of the required response as possible. The provision of advance information enables the guide dog to look ahead and produce a more fluent performance. Decisions in complex situations take time. *See also* ANTICIPATION, PERCEPTUAL ORGANIZATION, FILTERING and FLUENCY.

AFFECT – a wide range of emotions and states of arousal. Covers any aspect of feeling or emotional tone, as opposed to cognitive processes or behaviour. *See also* EMOTIONS.

ALARM REACTION – the physiological responses associated with activity of the sympathetic branch of the autonomic nervous system. The alarm reaction prepares the animal for fight or flight by increased blood pressure, heart rate and absorption and conversion of sugars etc. *See also* AUTONOMIC NERVOUS SYSTEM.

ANTHROPOCENTRISM – the belief that human beings are at the very centre of things. May result in the assumption animals are quite different from ourselves and lack the capacities for concept learning, problem solving and reasoning.

ANTHROPOMORPHISM – the attribution of human characteristics to animals and other nonhuman entities.

ANTICIPATION – a state of readiness for a specific event. If the guide dog is to overcome the problem of processing environmental information with a brain of 'limited processing capacity', it will have to operate within a 'framework of probabilities' about outcomes. In other words, it will have to learn to anticipate or predict what is likely to happen next.

The term is also used to refer to the unwanted anticipations (e.g. crossing a road diagonally, turning towards the park) that can occur in guide dog work.

ANXIETY – a stressful emotional or affective state resulting from the anticipation of danger or punishment.

Anxiety has:

> [i]   a physiological component in the form of the alarm or fight or flight reaction.
> [ii] a cognitive component that refers to the unpleasant arousal which results from fearful thoughts, anticipations, beliefs etc. that are related to specific objects, situations or events.

High levels of anxious arousal in the dog are considered to interfere with all aspects of skill learning and cognitive functioning. *See also* STRESS and LEARNED HELPLESSNESS.

ARTIFICIAL INTELLIGENCE (AI) – computer research concerned with getting computers to behave intelligently. *See also* INTELLIGENCE, ROBOTICS and TURING TEST.

ASSOCIATIVE LEARNING – learning which has resulted from the direct linking of a stimulus with a response. Pavlovian and operant conditioning are examples of associative learning procedures. Associative learning theorists, in the main, do not find it necessary to invoke mental processes (intervening between the stimulus and the response) to explain animal learning. *See also* STIMULUS-RESPONSE LEARNING.

ATTACHMENT – the secure relationship (tie or bond) which develops between mother and offspring, puppy and puppy walker, dog and trainer and GDO. The attachment figure (brood bitch, puppy walker, trainer, GDO) serve to buffer the pup or young dog against environmental stress and in turn the dog attempts to keep the attachment figure close (proximity seeking behaviour.) The quality of the attachments developed by the guide dog (during the puppy walking period and beyond) are likely to affect the dog's ability to be a confident and effective guide.

ATTENTION – a directed focusing of awareness, in preparation for responding to specific aspects of sensory input from the environment. In the case of the guide dog, to task relevant stimuli. Attention is a limited cognitive resource. *See also* CONSCIOUSNESS and SELECTIVE ATTENTION.

AUTOMATIC BEHAVIOUR – well practised responses which have been pushed from the forefront of consciousness and are now controlled by lower centres in the central nervous system. This down-grading allows the higher cognitive processes of decision making and problem solving to be applied to difficult or novel aspects of the environment. The efficiency of the guide dog's information processing capacity is heightened and the demand placed upon the sensory and effector functions is reduced. With practice, skill behaviour becomes less deliberate and more automatic. *See also* INFORMATION OVERLOAD and CHUNKING.

AUTONOMIC NERVOUS SYSTEM – a network of nerves which constitute the involuntary or visceral nervous system. The system has two main branches, the sympathetic and parasympathetic divisions. Activation of the sympathetic division prepares the animal for fight or flight and is a part of the physiological component of emotional reactions such as anxiety, fear and excitement. Activation of the parasympathetic division produces more quiescent and relaxed functioning of the body. Pavlovian conditioning is considered to be mediated via the autonomic nervous system. *See also* ALARM REACTION and ANXIETY.

AVOIDANCE LEARNING – an operant procedure where an aversive or punishing event is avoided by behaving in a specific way. As the animal is never sure whether the punishment will really occur, avoidance learning is very resistant to extinction. *See also* EXTINCTION.

BEHAVIOUR – movements or actions. *See also* MOTOR SKILL.

BEHAVIOUR SHAPING – an operant procedure where new behaviours are acquired through the systematic application of reinforcers. Once component responses are established, only those behaviours which approximate more closely to the final goal are reinforced. Shaping of new responses through the judicious use of positive reinforcers is a procedure which is fundamental to guide dog training. *See also* OPERANT LEARNING, POSITIVE REINFORCEMENT and POSITIVE REINFORCER.

BEHAVIOURISM – the school of psychology, founded by Watson (1913), which argued if psychology was to become a science it must study only behaviour that could be directly observed. Watson believed even human behaviour would eventually be understood as a process involving complex chains of stimulus-response connections. Behaviourism adopted an antimentalistic stance to the explanation of both human and animal behaviour. *See also* RADICAL BEHAVIOURISM. *Compare* NEO-BEHAVIOURISM.

BEHAVIOURIST – a psychologist who follows the main tenets of psychological investigation adopted by behaviourism.

BINARY DISTINCTION – the discrimination or decision that has to be made between two equally probable alternatives. The notion of a binary distinction is used in the book in relation to the number of decisions that have to be made by the guide dog in the complex task of road crossing. *See also* DISCRIMINATION, COMBINATORIAL EXPLOSION and INFORMATION OVERLOAD.

BOTTOM-UP PROCESSING – perceptual processing based on the characteristics of environmental stimuli. While perceptual and other cognitive processing is substantially affected by the nature of the incoming environmental data, it is also affected by context and the animal's past experience and expectations, i.e. by top-down processing. Perception is considered to be the result of the interaction of bottom-up processing (data driven) and top-down processing (concept driven). *See also* TOP-DOWN PROCESSING and PERCEPTION.

CATEGORIZATION – the process where stimulus objects are grouped together to form a class e.g. road vehicles, pedestrians, pavement obstacles. *See also* CONCEPT.

CENTRAL NERVOUS SYSTEM (CNS) – the network of nerve cells, fibres and support cells which form the brain and spinal cord. The CNS coordinates and regulates the major functions of the body including motor actions, perceptual and memory processes, thinking and reasoning. *See also* CEREBRAL CORTEX.

CEREBRAL CORTEX – the outer layer of the brain. It is in the grey matter of the cortex that higher level cognitive functions are thought to take place.

CHUNKING – a term introduced by Miller to account for how information may be grouped together in order to overcome processing constraints within the memory system.

The term chunking has been used in this book to refer to the related processes of:

[i]   Input chunking – the process where a whole series of stimuli or events are grouped together as a whole or pattern such that they are processed as a single unit of information. Greater efficiency on processing information on the input or sensory side produces greater efficiency on the output or motor side.

[ii]   Output chunking – the process of grouping together movement sequences. Motor fluency would seem to be brought about by two operations. Firstly, actions are integrated together into a single chunk which is then run off as a single unit of behaviour. Secondly, by the development of the capacity to overlap in time a sequence of movements with another. That is to say, preparation (and even movement itself) for one series of actions is commenced before a previous sequence of actions has been completed.

See also PERCEPTUAL ORGANIZATION, FILTERING and FLUENCY.

COGNITION – the higher mental processes of recognising, selecting, discriminating, remembering, predicting, organizing and making use of knowledge. The term cognition is used when the behaviour exhibited by the animal in response to environmental events is more than a predictable and automatic reaction. *See also* MIND and COGNITIVE PSYCHOLOGY.

COGNITIVE ETHOLOGY – the exploration of the mental experiences of animals, particularly within their natural environment. A field of study created by Griffin.

COGNITIVE MAP – a term introduced into psychology by Tolman (1932) to refer to an internal representation of an animal's environment. The map provides the basis on which the animal can form a plan to guide its behaviour. Tolman shocked his behaviourist colleagues by suggesting that even rats had the capacity to develop cognitive maps. Tolman was one of the first psychologists to demonstrate that cognition might be involved in animal learning. *See also* REPRESENTATION.

COGNITIVE PSYCHOLOGY – the branch of psychology concerned with the study of cognition i.e. the study of perception, attention, memory, imagery, language, concept learning, reasoning, problem solving, decision making etc. *See also* COGNITION and MIND.

COGNITIVE SKILL – an acquired set of mental abilities used to achieve a specified goal e.g. reasoning and problem solving. *Compare* MOTOR SKILL.

COMBINATORIAL EXPLOSION – used to refer to the rapid increase in the number of mental operations required of the guide dog to arrive at a 'safe decision' when it is presented with a complex situation in which there are a number of variables that need to be taken into account. *See also* BINARY DISTINCTION and INFORMATION OVERLOAD.

COMMAND – a directive issued to the dog which has to be immediately obeyed provided it is safe to do so. *Compare* GUIDING INSTRUCTION.

COMMONSENSE – used with the meaning:

[i]   first introduced into Western

philosophy by Aristotle i.e.as a general sense modality which integrates information from the five special senses;

[ii]   that there is a display of sound practical judgement.

CONCEPT – developed when objects are grouped together to form a class on the basis of their common characteristics. Concepts are mental representations which are acquired by learning and become part of the guide dog's top-down knowledge. *See also* CATEGORIZATION and OBJECT PERMANENCE.

CONDITIONED REFLEX – in Pavlovian conditioning the response acquired and given automatically to a previously neutral stimulus i.e. one that did not elicit the response prior to conditioning. An example of a conditioned reflex is the salivary response of a dog to a bell. The bell is the conditioned or conditional stimulus and salivation the conditioned or conditional response, the whole process constituting a conditioned reflex. *See also* CONDITIONING, PAVLOVIAN CONDITIONING and REFLEX.

CONDITIONING – the process of learning the relationship between stimuli and between stimuli and responses. Although the term should be strictly reserved for Pavlovian conditioning it is also used in relation to operant learning/conditioning.

CONFIDENCE QUADRANGLE – a model which proposes that the guide dog will need to develop for effective performance:

[i]   a confidence in itself;
[ii]   a confidence in its handler – puppy walker, instructor and GDO.

And in turn the handler must develop:

[i]   a confidence in the dog;
[ii]   a confidence in him or herself.

CONNECTIONISM – term used as equivalent to parallel distributed processing, so called because more than one input is involved in the formation of the connections within the modelled neural network. Connectionism (or PDP) has had a recent revival in the field of artificial intelligence. It is an approach that attempts to represent more accurately the activities taking place in real brains by constructing nerve nets. The brain processes most of its information in parallel. *See also* NERVE NET/NETWORK and PARALLEL PROCESSING.

CONSCIOUSNESS – an awareness of the external world by an animal or human and of their own behaviour. It is argued the guide dog has a conscious awareness of its environment and of what it is doing. *See also* MIND.

CONTEXT – the environmental setting in which a behaviour occurs. Context cues are of importance for decision making by the guide dog. *See also* ENVIRONMENT.

DECISION – the choice between alternative courses of action. Viewing the guide dog primarily as a decision maker is a theme developed throughout the book. *See also* REASONING and PROBLEM SOLVING.

DECLARATIVE KNOWLEDGE/MEMORY – knowing what to do as opposed to knowing how to do something (procedural knowledge). The term is used to refer to the knowledge gained by the guide dog about the 'what' of the guiding task. Knowledge about what to do is being acquired by the guide dog at the same time as knowledge about how to do it. *See also* PROCEDURAL KNOWLEDGE.

DECODING – translating information into a form that can be understood.

DETOUR PROBLEM – any problem in which to reach a goal an animal or human has initially to move in an alternative direction to get round an obstacle blocking its route. *See also* GOAL, THINKING, INSIGHT LEARNING and PROBLEM SOLVING.

DISCRIMINATION – the ability to perceive a difference between two or more stimuli. The guide dog has to learn to discriminate between many complex stimulus events in its work – multiple discrimination learning. *See also* BINARY DISTINCTION, CATEGORIZATION and PATTERN RECOGNITION.

DOMINANCE-SUBMISSION CONFLICT – a dilemma experienced by the guide dog of knowing in which situations to be submissive to the handler and in which to use its initiative and take responsibility. The resolution of this conflict is significant for the work. When in harness (and with the handle raised) the guide dog is, for the most part, having to take the guiding decisions and it is essential the decisions it takes are supported by the instructor and GDO.

EFFECTOR SYSTEM – *see* MOTOR SYSTEM.

EFFORT AFTER MEANING – phrase introduced by Bartlett to describe the attempt to give meaning to material both in perception and from memory. *See also* PERCEPTION and TOP-DOWN PROCESSING.

EMOTIONS – a wide range of pleasurable (positive) and uncomfortable (negative) feelings. Most emotions are considered to have:

    [i] A physiological component associated with activity of the autonomic or involuntary nervous system.

    [ii] A cognitive component associated with the organism's (animal or human) reading of the situation.

A cognitive account of emotions would view physiological activity as secondary to the organism's appraisal of the situation. *See also* ANXIETY.

ENVIRONMENT – the total external context in which an animal or human operates. *See also* CONTEXT.

ETHOLOGY – originally referred to the study of animals in their natural environment, with emphasis upon innate and evolutionary processes to explain their behaviour. *See also* INNATE and COGNITIVE ETHOLOGY.

EXPECTANCIES – the anticipation of certain consequences associated with a particular act or set of environmental events in a specific context. *See also* CONDITIONING, ANTICIPATION and PREDICTION.

EXTINCTION – the reduction in the strength of a learned response that occurs when the stimulus controlling it is repeatedly presented without a reinforcer being given. A term used in relation to both operant and Pavlovian conditioning. *Compare* HABITUATION.

FAR TRAFFIC – vehicles travelling in the lane furthest away from the guide dog team when at the kerb edge. *Compare* NEAR TRAFFIC.

FEATURE ANALYSIS – an explanation of pattern recognition in which elemental features of an object are combined in the brain during the process of perception. *See also* PATTERN RECOGNITION, PERCEPTION AND SCHEMA. *Compare* TEMPLATE-MATCHING THEORY and PROTOTYPE THEORY.

FEEDBACK INFORMATION – information

about the effect or outcome of a course of behaviour enacted by an animal or human. Feedback information is essential for skill acquisition by the guide dog.

Four different forms of feedback may be identified in the process of skill acquisition.

> [i] Action feedback – information received through the senses about the progress of a sequence of behaviours. Provided the guide dog knows what it is expected to do in any particular situation, action feedback can be used by the dog for self-correction.

> [ii] Extrinsic feedback – information given by the handler to the guide dog through the delivery of appropriately timed reinforcers e.g. praise. Behaviour is shaped and maintained in this way.

> [iii] Learning feedback – information received through the senses about the outcome of a particular sequence of behaviours e.g. knowledge of the successful completion of a manoeuvre to avoid a pavement obstacle.

> [iv] Proprioceptive feedback – information received from the muscles, tendons and joints about the position of the body and limbs.

See also TOTE CYCLE.

FILTERING – the process where incoming sensory information is channelled such that only a selected part of it is received centrally. Without a filtering system, the guide dog would be subjected continually to the possibility of 'information overload'. All brains are limited to the amount of information they can process during a set period of time. *See also* CHUNKING (especially input chunking), SELECTIVE ATTENTION,

INFORMATION OVERLOAD and PERCEPTUAL ORGANIZATION.

FLUENCY – specifically used in this book to refer to the relaxed smoothness and coordinated flow of the guide dog team's movements. Fluency is acquired late in the development of a skill and breaks down rapidly under stress. *See also* CHUNKING.

FOREBRAIN – the most recently evolved part of the brain and is of particular importance in the integration and organization of information and behaviour.

GDO – Guide Dog Owner.

GESTALT – used by the gestalt school of psychology to indicate that a stimulus configuration is more than the sum of its parts. The literal translation from the German is 'essence' or 'form'.

GESTALT PSYCHOLOGY – a school of psychology, under the leadership of Koffka, Kohler and Wertheimer, which questioned the mechanistic and atomistic approach of the school of behaviourism to the explanation of human and animal behaviour. Gestalt psychology stressed the holistic nature of psychological processes and opposed stimulus-response reductionism – "The whole is more than the sum of its parts". *Compare* BEHAVIOURISM.

GOAL – the aim or desirable end point of a behavioural or mental activity. *See also* SKILL, REASONING and PROBLEM SOLVING.

GUIDE DOG TEAM – the working partnership of guide dog and guide dog owner.

GUIDED LEARNING – the process of 'showing' the dog the nature of a required behaviour sequence by use of the leash, gesture, vocal prompts and body position.

GUIDING INSTRUCTION – a request issued to the guide dog to take a guiding action when in the correct position to comply e.g. "find left", "find door". *Compare* COMMAND.

HABIT – a learned stimulus-response sequence of behaviours.

HABITUATION – the weakening of an unlearned response by repeated exposure to the stimulus which evokes it. The guide dog will need to habituate to many stimuli that are without significance for it within the context of the guiding task. Habituation reduces the dangers of distraction and of overloading the dog's cognitive system with irrelevant information. *See also* FILTERING and INFORMATION OVERLOAD.

HARDWARE – a computer term used to refer to the physical apparatus on which software programs are run. The neurophysiological structure of the brain may be equated with computer hardware. *Compare* SOFTWARE.

HELPLESSNESS – *see* LEARNED HELPLESSNESS.

HIERARCHY – used very broadly in many areas of psychology.

It has been used in this book in relation to:

> [i]   The hierarchical organization of the operate phase within the TOTE cycle. It is suggested (Annett, 1969) that the operate phase of the TOTE cycle could be expanded hierarchically to include any number of subordinate TOTE units.

> [ii]   The hierarchical organization of skilled action where well-practised responses are down-graded and taken over by lower centres in the central nervous system.

See also TOTE CYCLE and AUTOMATIC BEHAVIOUR.

IMAGE – *see* REPRESENTATION.

INFORMATION OVERLOAD – the state of having too much information with which to deal in a given period of time. The guide dog is vulnerable to 'information overload' (which may often produce stress) during the early period of training or when working in novel or difficult conditions. Anxiety (whatever its cause) will reduce the dog's information processing capacity. *See also* FILTERING, CHUNKING and FLUENCY.

INFORMATION PROCESSING SYSTEM – the guide dog is viewed as an information processing system. An information processing framework has proved to be a valuable approach for the study of attention, perception, decision making, skill learning etc. Environmental information has to be attended to selectively, recognized for what it is and used to guide motor output. However, it is a model that can still conveniently avoid attributing to the dog a capacity for conscious awareness.

INHERIT – the acquisition of characteristics through genetic transmission. *See also* INNATE.

INNATE – unlearned and present at birth.

INPUT – information fed into a computer or the data received by the sense organs. *See also* OUTPUT and CHUNKING.

INSIGHT LEARNING – used by the gestalt psychologist Kohler to describe the sudden and complete solution of a problem through a mental restructuring. Insight learning would seem to necessitate the animal being able to form a mental representation of the problem and have a grasp of the goal to be achieved. Kohler's account of animal learning contrasted sharply with the views of Thorndike and other behaviourists. *See also*

DETOUR PROBLEM, GESTALT PSYCHOLOGY and BEHAVIOURISM. *Compare* TRIAL AND ERROR LEARNING.

INSTINCT – an unlearned complex pattern of behaviour which is common to all members of a species. *See also* ETHOLOGY and INNATE.

INTELLIGENCE – one of the most problematic concepts to define. Used in the book to refer to the dog's ability to learn, think and understand. It relates to the quality and complexity of the dog's cognitive functioning. *See also* COGNITION, LEARNING, THINKING and MIND.

INVOLUNTARY NERVOUS SYSTEM – a network of nerves which regulate those activities of the body which are not under cortical control. *See also* AUTONOMIC NERVOUS SYSTEM.

LEARNED HELPLESSNESS – an experimentally induced inability of dogs to escape from an electric shock after first being administered a series of inescapable shocks. It seemed the dogs had come to 'believe' their actions were of no use in preventing or escaping the shock – they had learned to be helpless. The dog that has learned to be `helpless' (for whatever reason) may show cognitive deficits, stress related disorders and a reduction in its will to learn. *See also* ANXIETY, ANTICIPATION and PREDICTION.

LEARNING – the more or less permanent change in behaviour and knowledge as a result of experience, as opposed to change due to innate mechanisms, maturation, drugs, illness or fatigue. The skills displayed by the guide dog are acquired by learning. *See also* SKILL, ACQUISITION and ADAPTATION. *Compare* MATURATION.

LINEAR PROCESSING – *see* SERIAL PROCESSING.

MATURATION – age related physical and behavioural changes caused by genetic action that cannot be attributed to learning. Since age related physical and behavioural changes are the product of an interaction between environmental and genetic forces, it is perhaps misleading to restrict the term maturation to the effects of genetic influences alone. More needs to be known about the ages at which the dog most efficiently acquires specific behaviours pertinent to the guiding task. *Compare* LEARNING.

MEMORY – the general term given to the store of information acquired by an animal or human as a result of experience. Throughout training (and beyond) the guide dog is storing information about the guiding task; knowledge about stimulus objects and events and rules of response associated with their occurrence. *See also* DECLARATIVE KNOWLEDGE/MEMORY and PROCEDURAL KNOWLEDGE/MEMORY.

MENTALISTIC – refers to internal cognitive processes in the mind or brain.

MIND – used in the book to refer to the totality of mental processes of the brain. Mind is a process and not a thing. The processes involved in perception, memory and other aspects of cognition collectively constitute the mind. A mental process is a cognitive process. *See also* COGNITION and CONSCIOUSNESS.

MOTIVATION – the internal energizing forces for goal-directed behaviour. In the context of guide dog work, the emphasis is upon the dog's willingness to work and learn.

MOTOR SKILL – those skills concerned with the regulation of muscular movement. All motor skills have a cognitive component involved in the co-ordination and organization of the sensory (input) and effector (output) systems. The cognitive component of a motor skill operates as a central regulating system. It is motor skills that are acquired by the guide dog during training and beyond. *See also* SKILL. *Compare* COGNITIVE SKILL.

MOTOR SYSTEM – all parts of the nervous system that control muscles and the movements they bring about. *See also* MOTOR SKILL.

NEAR TRAFFIC – vehicles travelling in the lane closest to the guide dog team when at the kerb edge. *Compare* FAR TRAFFIC.

NEO-BEHAVIOURISM – any form of behaviourism after Watson. Usually thought of as a more reasonable form of behaviourism which accepts that cognitive processes have a role to play in the determination and explanation of behaviour e.g. Tolman's purposive or cognitive behaviourism. *See also* BEHAVIOURISM and COGNITIVE ETHOLOGY.

NEOTENIZE – to retain youthful and playful behaviour. We have selectively bred to retain playfulness in our dogs and need to capitalize on the dog's ability to learn through play.

NERVE CELL – *see* NEURONE.

NERVE NET/NETWORK – a complex series of units which both activate and inhibit one another through their interconnections. *See also* ARTIFICIAL INTELLIGENCE and CONNECTIONISM.

NEUROBIOLOGY – the study of the nervous system and its role in behaviour and cognition.

NEURONE – a nerve cell which transmits information.

NEUROSCIENCE – all disciplines eg. neurobiology, neuroanatomy, neurophysiology that seek to understand the relationship between the nervous system and behaviour.

OBJECT PERMANENCE – the knowledge developed by a child that an object continues to exist even when it passes out of sight. *See also* CONCEPT and THINKING.

OBSERVATIONAL LEARNING – the acquisition of behaviour through observing the behaviour of others.

OPERANT CONDITIONING/LEARNING – a process of learning where a spontaneous voluntary response emitted by an animal or human is strengthened or weakened as a result of the stimulus events that follow that response. Operant learning procedures are fundamental to guide dog training and skill acquisition. However, it is the manner in which operant procedures are applied that is crucial. *See also* CONDITIONING and BEHAVIOUR SHAPING. *Compare* PAVLOVIAN CONDITIONING.

OUTPUT – information produced by a computer or the behaviour of an animal or human in response to an input. *See also* INPUT and CHUNKING.

PARALLEL PROCESSING – the carrying out of more than one process at a time either by a computer or a brain. Most operations within the brain are executed in parallel. *See also* CONNECTIONISM. *Compare* SERIAL PROCESSING.

PATTERN RECOGNITION – the process of identifying that a particular array of stimulus elements represents a particular class of objects e.g. identifying a dog is a dog and not a cat. *See also* CONCEPT, CATEGORIZATION, TEMPLATE-MATCHING THEORY, FEATURE ANALYSIS, PROTOTYPE THEORY and PROSOPAGNOSIA.

PAVLOVIAN CONDITIONING – the pairing of a previously neutral stimulus (e.g. a whistle) with a stimulus which reliably produces a response (e.g.

food) such that the neutral stimulus produces the same (or similar) response when presented alone (in this case salivation). The neutral stimulus becomes the conditional stimulus (CS) and the response to that stimulus the conditional response (CR). Pavlovian conditioning is considered to be passive and mediated via the involuntary or autonomic nervous system. *See also* CONDITIONED REFLEX and CONDITIONING. *Compare* OPERANT CONDITIONING/ LEARNING.

PERCEPTION – the active cognitive process that makes incoming sensory data meaningful. It thus refers to the way information from the environment is transformed into experiences of objects and events. Perception may be distinguished from sensation which is the stimulation of the sensory receptors. Some workers (e.g. Neisser) view perception as synonymous with cognition in general. *See also* COGNITION, BOTTOM-UP PROCESSING and TOP-DOWN PROCESSING.

PERCEPTUAL ORGANIZATION – the process where incoming sensory data is categorized, such that objects are recognized and the information efficiently processed. Used in the book to account for the guide dog's gradually acquired capacity to organize information so that even the most complex sequences of task significant data can be effectively handled. The dog comes to operate within a 'framework of probabilities' in which it looks ahead and predicts outcomes. *See also* CHUNKING, FILTERING, SELECTIVE ATTENTION and PROBABILITY.

PHYSICAL PUNISHMENT – used within the context of guide dog training to refer to a handle or chain check. *See also* PUNISHMENT. *Compare* VERBAL PUNISHMENT.

PLANNED ACTION – used in the book to refer to the guide dog's ability to realise short and long range goals within the rules of the guiding task. *See also* PURPOSIVE BEHAVIOUR, TOTE CYCLE and PROBLEM SOLVING.

POSITIVE REINFORCEMENT – the process where the strength and frequency of a response is increased by following that response with a positive reinforcer e.g. praise. *See also* POSITIVE REINFORCER.

POSITIVE REINFORCER – a stimulus that when applied following a response increases the strength and frequency of that response. The defining characteristic of a positive reinforcer is that it increases the frequency and strength of the response it follows. *See also* POSITIVE REINFORCEMENT.

PRACTICE – the repetition of an act or a series of acts for the improvement of a skill. *See also* LEARNING, SKILL and MOTOR SKILL.

PREDICTION – the acquired ability to anticipate outcomes within the context of skilled action. *See also* ANTICIPATION (synonym in the context of skill performance.)

PROBABILITY – the likelihood that an event will occur. Used in relation to the development of a 'framework of probabilities' by the guide dog. *See also* ANTICIPATION, PREDICTION and PERCEPTUAL ORGANIZATION.

PROBLEM SOLVING – the cognitive activity where a difficulty is overcome and a desired goal is attained. Many (but certainly not all) of the situations faced by the guide dog would appear to require a form of problem solving, especially when working in difficult or novel areas. *See also* REASONING and INSIGHT LEARNING.

PROCEDURAL KNOWLEDGE/MEMORY – knowing how to do something, as opposed to knowing what to do. The procedural knowledge acquired by the guide dog is represented internally as a set of motor responses associated with a class of stimulus objects or events. *See also* MOTOR SKILL. *Compare* DECLARATIVE KNOWLEDGE/MEMORY.

PROCESS – any activity that produces an outcome.

PROGRAM – a set of instructions to a computer to carry out a specified set of operations. *See also* SOFTWARE.

PROSOPAGNOSIA – a clinical condition in which a person is unable to recognize faces because of damage to nerve cells in the temporal lobe of the brain. It may be congenital or the result of a stroke or disease. *See also* PATTERN RECOGNITION and PERCEPTION.

PROTOTYPE THEORY – a theory of pattern recognition in which the incoming sensory data is compared with an abstract representation of the stimulus object. These abstract forms, called prototypes, represent the most basic and essential elements of the stimulus object. Every stimulus has characteristics which define its class membership. *See also* PERCEPTION, SCHEMA and PATTERN RECOGNITION. *Compare* TEMPLATE-MATCHING THEORY and FEATURE ANALYSIS.

PSYCHOLOGY – many definitions are possible, but it can be described as, 'The scientific study of human and animal behaviour and mental processes.'

PUNISHMENT – in general, any event that an animal or human seeks to escape or avoid. More precisely, punishment is a stimulus that when applied reduces the strength and frequency of the response it follows. *See also* PHYSICAL PUNISHMENT and VERBAL PUNISHMENT.

PURPOSIVE BEHAVIOUR – refers in the book to the intentional and systematic behaviour of the guide dog as it operates to a plan in the pursuit of short and long range goals. *See also* CONSCIOUSNESS, GOAL, PROBLEM SOLVING and PLANNED ACTION.

PUZZLE BOX – an apparatus, designed by Thorndike, containing some form of locking and opening device. An animal when placed in the box has to discover how to escape from it to obtain a reward. *See also* SKINNER BOX and TRIAL AND ERROR LEARNING.

RADICAL BEHAVIOURISM – a form of behaviourism espoused by Skinner and others in which any causative role for cognitive processes is denied. *See also* REDUCTIONISM.

REASONING – used in the book to refer to the process where the guide dog combines two or more sets of information in order to reach a satisfactory goal. *See also* PROBLEM SOLVING and THINKING.

RECEPTOR – used mainly to refer to a sense receptor i.e. a cell or group of cells which is structured to pick up sensory information and convert it into electrical energy for transmission to the central nervous system. The sense receptors are designed to receive information from the outside world (exteroceptors), from the organs of the body (interoceptors) and from the muscles, tendons and joints (proprioceptors). *See also* CHUNKING, FILTERING and SENSE ORGAN.

REDUCTIONISM – a form of argument (or even doctrine) that suggests that a behaviour, phenomenon or event can be explained by reference to its most simple components e.g. that animal or human behaviour can be explained as a set of stimulus-response connections without reference to higher cognitive processes. *See also* BEHAVIOURISM, RADICAL BEHAVIOURISM and GESTALT PSYCHOLOGY.

REFLEX – an involuntary, automatic and

mechanical response elicited by a stimulus without the involvement of higher cerebral processes. *See also* PAVLOVIAN CONDITIONING.

REINFORCEMENT – *see* POSITIVE REINFORCEMENT.

REPRESENTATION – a mental image (visual, olfactory, auditory, spatial) formed in the brain of stimulus objects and events. A cognitive map is an example of a complex mental representation. *See also* COGNITIVE MAP and SCHEMA.

ROBOTICS – study of how to get computer controlled machines to perform mechanical tasks similar to those performed by a human being. *See also* ARTIFICIAL INTELLIGENCE.

SCHEMA – a hypothetical model or construct for describing how knowledge is stored by the brain. A schema may be thought of as a mental representation. *See also* MEMORY, REPRESENTATION and PROTOTYPE THEORY.

SELECTIVE ATTENTION – the concentration on a stimulus or class of events to the exclusion of others. Attention is a limited cognitive resource and it is essential for the guide dog to attend to task relevant stimuli and events. *See also* FILTERING, HABITUATION and INFORMATION OVERLOAD.

SENSE ORGAN – any specialized set of nerve cells that respond to a particular class of stimulation. *See also* RECEPTOR.

SERIAL PROCESSING – the carrying out of one process at a time. Serial processing of information occurs in a series of consecutive steps. Early models of information processing by the brain were couched in terms of serial or linear processing (e.g. Broadbent, 1958). Brains operate mainly in parallel. *See also* CONNECTIONISM. *Compare* PARALLEL PROCESSING.

SHAPING – *see* BEHAVIOUR SHAPING.

SKILL – a learned and complex pattern of motor or cognitive behaviours directed towards the attainment of a specific goal. Two of the defining criteria of a skill are that the behaviours are both learned and complex. *See also* COGNITIVE SKILL, MOTOR SKILL and ABILITY.

SKINNER BOX – an apparatus, designed by Skinner, containing a lever or some other form of device that can be pressed or pecked by an animal to deliver a food reward or other form of stimulus. The responses of the animal can be recorded automatically. *See also* PUZZLE BOX.

SOFTWARE – a computer program as opposed to the physical components of a computer. Software programs are run on the hardware. The activities of the brain may be equated with software programs and the structure of the brain thought of as the hardware. *See also* PROGRAM. *Compare* HARDWARE.

STIMULUS – any pattern of stimulation that impinges upon sense receptors to produce a response. *See also* RECEPTOR, PERCEPTION and STIMULUS DISCRIMINATION.

STIMULUS DISCRIMINATION – the learned ability of an animal to respond to one stimulus but not to another that is similar e.g. the response of a dog to a whistle of a particular frequency, but not to another whistle of a similar frequency. *See also* DISCRIMINATION.

STIMULUS-RESPONSE LEARNING – the learning of an association between a stimulus and some form of behavioural response. Pavlovian and Skinnerian conditioning represent the two main forms of stimulus-response learning. *See also* ASSOCIATIVE LEARNING, BEHAVIOURISM, CONDITIONING and REFLEX. *Compare* INSIGHT LEARNING.

STRESS – the effect of being subjected to an aversive event or the anticipation of such an event. The guide dog is particularly vulnerable to stress when unable to reduce or terminate the uncomfortable level of noxious stimulation. Information overload may also produce stress reactions in the dog when working in difficult conditions. A positively orientated training regime (with a consequent reduction in the use of physical punishment) will reduce significantly the level of stress experienced by the guide dog. *See also* ANXIETY, LEARNED HELPLESSNESS and INFORMATION OVERLOAD.

TEMPLATE-MATCHING THEORY – a theory which attempts to explain pattern recognition by supposing patterns are recognized by matching them to an identical image. As explained in the text, the theory fails as an adequate explanation of pattern recognition. *See also* PERCEPTION. *Compare* FEATURE ANALYSIS and PROTOTYPE THEORY.

THINKING – a general term referring to cognitive processes concerned with problem solving. Thinking is dependent upon two mental abilities:

> [i]   the ability to represent the world inside the head;

> [ii]   the ability to manipulate mental representations to predict the likely outcome of a particular course of action.

See also INTELLIGENCE, COGNITION and REASONING.

TOP-DOWN PROCESSING – the perceptual processing which is affected by what the animal or human brings to a particular stimulus situation e.g. expectations governed by context and past experience, concepts and world knowledge. Perception is considered to be the result of the interaction of bottom-up processing (data driven) and top-down processing (concept driven). *See also* BOTTOM-UP PROCESSING, PERCEPTION and EFFORT AFTER MEANING.

TOTE CYCLE – an abbreviation for Test-Operate-Test-Exit. Adapted from the work of Miller, Galanter and Pribram to account for planned action by the guide dog. It is proposed the dog tests the environment; operates to bring about the necessary change; tests again to check whether the situation is in accord with the intended state of affairs, and if it is, exits from the cycle. *See also* HIERARCHY, PLANNED ACTION and PURPOSIVE BEHAVIOUR.

TRIAL AND ERROR LEARNING – a type of learning described by Thorndike in which the animal tries out a number of responses to a given stimulus until it accidentally hits upon one which produces the desired effect. The response which produces the desired outcome is presumed to be strengthened and gradually 'stamped in' over a number of trials. Thorndike assumed that learning was the result of direct stimulus-response connections. *See also* OPERANT CONDITIONING/LEARNING, STIMULUS-RESPONSE LEARNING and PUZZLE BOX. *Compare* INSIGHT LEARNING.

TURING TEST – a hypothetical test devised by Turing to test whether or not an artificial intelligence in the form of a computer system can think in the same way as a human being. A person is asked to interrogate and communicate with another person or a computer system. Both are hidden from view and both use the same form of communication e.g. printed material. The test is whether the person can tell to which he or she is connected. No artificial intelligence has yet been designed that could pass the Turing test. *See also* ARTIFICIAL INTELLIGENCE and ROBOTICS.

VERBAL PUNISHMENT – any vocal stimulus that

when applied by the instructor or GDO reduces the strength or frequency of the response it follows. *See also* PHYSICAL PUNISHMENT and PUNISHMENT.

VOLUNTARY BEHAVIOUR – a behaviour which is intended by the animal. Compare involuntary behaviour as typically acquired by Pavlovian conditioning procedures.

Bibliography

Aitkenhead, A.M. and Slack, J.M. eds. (1985) *Issues in cognitive modelling*. London: LEA.

Alexsander, I. and Morton, H. (1993) *Neurons and symbols: the stuff that mind is made of.* Chapman and Hall.

Anderson, J.R. (1980) *Cognitive psychology and its implications.* San Francisco, Freeman.

Anderson, J.R. (1983) *The architecture of cognition.* Cambridge MA: Harvard University Press.

Annett, J. (1969) *Feedback and human performance.* Harmondsworth: Penguin.

Austin, T. *Dog Psychology.* In The Australian Kelpie Handbook (1985). N. Macleod.

Baars, B.J. (1988) *A cognitive theory of consciousness.* Cambridge: Cambridge University Press.

Bandura, A. (1986) *Social foundations of thought and action: a social cognitive theory.* NJ: Prentice Hall Inc.

Bartlett, F.C. (1932) *Remembering: a study in experimental and social psychology.* Cambridge: Cambridge University Press.

Bartlett, F.C. (1948) *The measurement of human skill.* Occupational Psychology 22.

Blakemore, C. and Cooper, G.F. (1970) *Development of the brain depends on the visual environment.* Nature, 228.

Boden, M.A. (1988) *Computer models of mind.* Cambridge: Cambridge University Press.

Boden, M.A. (1989) *Artificial intelligence in psychology: interdisciplinary essays.* Cambridge MA: MIT Press.

Bruner, J.S., Jolly A. and Sylva, K. (1976) *Play, its role in development and evolution.* Penguin.

Bruner, J.S. *The importance of play.* In Child alive: new insights into the development of young children. (1975) R. Lewin. Maurice Smith Ltd.

Chapuis, N., Thinus-Blanc, C. and Poucet, B. (1983) *Dissociation of mechanisms involved in dogs' oriented displacements.* Quarterly Journal of Experimental Psychology 35B.

Cohen, G. (1983) *The psychology of cognition.* 2nd. ed. London Academic Press.

Cohen, G. (1989) *Memory in the real world.* Hove and London: LEA.

Craig-Head, W.E., Kazdin, A.G. and Mahoney, M.J. (1981) *Behaviour modification: principles, issues and practice.* Boston: Houghton Miffler.

Craik K. (1943) *The nature of explanation.* Cambridge: Cambridge University Press.

Crick, F. and Koch, C. *The problem of consciousness.* In Scientific American, September 1992.

Crossman, E.R.F.W. (1964) *Information processes in human skill.* British Medical Bulletin, 20.

Dennett, D.C. (1991) *Consciousness explained.* Penguin.

Dickinson, A. (1980) *Contemporary animal learning theory.* London: Cambridge University Press.

Eysenck, M.W. and Keane, M.T (1990) *Cognitive psychology: a student's handbook.* Hove and London: LEA.

Fischbach, G.D. *Mind and brain.* In Scientific American, September 1992.

Fogle, B. (1990) *The dog's mind.* Pelham.

Foulke, E. (1970) *The perceptual basis of mobility.* American Foundation for the Blind: Research Bulletin 23.

Freeman, D. (1991) *Barking up the right tree*. Ring Press Books Ltd.

Gardner, H. (1987) *The mind's new science: a history of the cognitive revolution*. Basic Books.
Gellatly, A. (1986) *The skilful mind: an introduction to cognitive psychology*. Milton Keynes: Open University Press.
Griffin, D.R. (1976) *The question of animal awareness*. New York Rockefeller University Press.
Griffin, D.R. (1984) *Animal thinking*. Cambridge MA: Harvard University Press.
Griffin, D.R. *Progress toward a cognitive ethology. In Cognitive Ethology: the minds of other animals*, C.A. Ristau (1991) L. Erlbaum, U.S.
Griffin, D.R. (1992) *Animals minds*. Chicago: University of Chicago Press.

Halliday, T.R. and Slater, P.G.B. eds. (1983) *Animal behaviour: genes, development and learning*: Vol. 3. Blackwell Science Publications.
Herrnstein, R.J. *Objects, categories and discriminating stimuli*. In Animal Cognition, H.L. Roitblat et al (1984). London: LEA.
Hinton, G.E. *How neural networks learn from experience*. In Scientific American, September 1992.
Holding, D. ed. (1989) *Human skills. 2nd. ed.* Chichester: John Wiley and Sons.
Hubel, D.H. and Wiesel, T.N. (1962) *Receptive fields, binocular interaction and functional architecture in the cat's visual cortex*. Journal of Physiology (London) 156.
Hubel, D.H. and Wiesel, T.N. (1968) *Receptive fields and functional architecture of monkey striate cortex*. Journal of Physiology (London) 195.

Johnson-Laird, P.N. (1988) *The computer and the mind: an introduction to cognitive science*. London: Fontana.
Johnston, B. (1990) *The skilful mind of the guide dog: towards a cognitive and holistic model of training*. GDBA.

Kahney, H. (1986) *Problem solving: a cognitive approach*. Open University Press.
Kohler, W. (1925) *The mentality of apes*. Harmondsworth: Penguin.

Lewin, R. (1975) *Child alive: new insights into the development of young children*. Maurice Temple Smith Ltd.

Mackintosh, N.J. (1974) *The psychology of animal learning*. London: Academic Press.
Mackintosh, N.J. (1983) *Conditioning and associative learning*. Oxford: Oxford University Press.
Marcel, A.J. eds., Bisiach, E. (1988) *Consciousness in contemporary science*. Oxford University Press.
Michel, G.F. *Human psychology and the minds of other animals*. In Cognitive Ethology: the minds of other animals, C.A. Ristau (1991). L. Erlbaum, U.S.
Miller, G.A., Galanter, E. and Pribram, K.H. (1960) *Plans and the structure of behaviour*. Holt, Rinehart and Winston.

Norman, D.A. *Twelve issues for cognitive science*. In Issues in cognitive modelling, A.M. Aitkenhead and J.M. Slack (1985). London: LEA.

Oakley, D.A. (1985) *Brain and mind*. London: Methuen.
O'Farrell, V. (1989) *Problem dog: behaviour and misbehaviour*. London: Metheuen.

Pavlov, I.P. (1927) *Conditioned reflexes*. New York: Oxford University Press.

Pavlov, I.P. (1955) *Selected works.* Moscow: Foreign Languages Publishing House.

Pearce, J.M. (1987) *An introduction to animal cognition.* Hove and London: LEA.

Piaget, J. (1973) *The child's conception of the world.* London: Paladin.

Premack, D. (1976) *Intelligence in ape and man.* Hillsdale NJ: LEA.

Premack, D. (1986) *Gavagai! Or the future of the animal learning controversy.* Cambridge MA: MIT Press.

Penguin (1989) *A dictionary of psychology.* Penguin.

Ristau, C.A. ed. (1990) *Cognitive ethology: the minds of other animals – essays in honour of Donald R. Griffen.* L. Erlbaum US.

Roitblat H.L. et al. eds. (1984) *Animal cognition.* London: LEA.

Roth, I. and Frisby, J.P. (1989) *Perception and representation. A cognitive approach.* Open University Press.

Salmoni, A.W. *Motor skill learning.* In Human Skills 2nd. ed., D. Holding (1989). Chichester: John Wiley and Sons.

Seligman, M.E.P. (1972) *Biological boundaries of learning.* New York: Appleton-Century-Crofts.

Seligman, M.E.P. and Maier, S.F. (1967) *Failure to escape traumatic shock.* Journal of Experimental Psychology 74.

Shingledecker, C.A. *Handicap and human skill.* In Human Skills 2nd. ed.,D. Holding (1989). Chichester: John Wiley and Sons.

Skinner, B.F. (1953) *Science and human behaviour.* New York: Macmillan.

Skinner, B.F. (1981) *Selection by consequences.* Science, 213.

Stamp Dawkins, M. (1993) *Through our eyes only? The search for animal consciousness.* W.H. Freeman.

Sutherland, S. (1991) *Macmillan Dictionary of Psychology.* Macmillan Press.

Taylor, A. et al eds. (1980) *Introducing psychology, 2nd ed.* Harmondsworth: Penguin.

Terrace, H.S. *Animal cognition.* In Animal Cognition, H.L. Roitblat (1994). London: LEA.

Thorndike, E.L. (1911) *Animal intelligence.* New York: Macmillan.

Tolman, E.C. (1932) *Purposive behaviour in animals and man.* New York: Century.

Tolman, E.C., Ritchie and B.F. Kalish, D. (1946) *Studies in spatial learning.* Journal of Experimental Psychology 36.

Walker, S. (1983) *Animal thought.* London: Routledge and Kegan Paul.

Watson, J.B. (1930) *Behaviourism.* (Republished 1970 – The Norton Library) New York: Norton and Company Inc.

Welford, A.J. (1976) *Skilled performance: perceptual and motor skills.* New York: Scott, Foresman.

Yoerg, S.I. and Kamil, A.C. *Integrating cognitive ethology with cognitive psychology.* In Cognitive Ethology: the minds of other animals, C.A. Ristau (1991) L. Erlbaum, U.S.

Zeki, S. *The visual image in mind and brain.* In Scientific American, September 1992.

Index

Page reference in bold type denotes glossary entry.